HOW TO GET WHAT YOU WANT

The secrets of reaching your goals in work, love and life

—

Patsy Westcott

BLOOMSBURY

This book is for my daughters Lucy and Kate
– may they get what they want

I would like to thank the following people who have helped me to write this book: Anna Clements, Lisa Robson, Nicola Gibson. I would also like to thank Jane Garton, editor of *Top Santé*, for her forbearance in my absence while I was writing it; Rowena Gaunt and Isabelle Auden at Bloomsbury.

Also available by Patsy Westcott
THE SURVIVOR PERSONALITY

The author and publisher of this book cannot be held responsible for any errors and omissions, or actions that may be taken as a consequence of using it.

All rights reserved: no part of this publication may be reproduced, stored in a retrieval system, or transmitted in any form or by any means, electronic, mechanical, photocopying or otherwise, without the prior written permission of the publisher.

First published 1995 by Bloomsbury Publishing Plc, 2 Soho Square, London, W1V 6HB

Copyright © 1995 Patsy Westcott

The moral right of the author has been asserted

A copy of the CIP entry for this book is available from the British Library

ISBN 0 7475 2159 X

10 9 8 7 6 5 4 3 2 1

Designed by Hugh Adams, AB3
Typeset by Hewer Text Composition Services, Edinburgh
Printed in Britain by Cox & Wyman Ltd, Reading

CONTENTS

On a personal note   v

PART ONE – THE BASIC PLAN
Introduction   1
Chapter one   4
    Defining what you want
Chapter two   19
    Getting going
Chapter three   30
    Turning your dreams into reality
Chapter four   42
    Time for a change
Chapter five   56
    Conjuring the cash
Chapter six   70
    Talking about what you want
Chapter seven   88
    Avoiding the trip wires

PART TWO – MAKING THINGS HAPPEN
Introduction   109
Chapter eight   110
    Getting the work you want
Chapter nine   126
    Getting the relationship you want
Chapter ten   148
    Looking the way you want

Chapter eleven 161
    Living a long and healthy life
Chapter twelve 180
    It's your life
Chapter thirteen 186
    You can't always get what you want
Chapter fourteen 194
    This is just the beginning

PART THREE – INSPIRATIONS
Chapter fifteen 201
    Inspiring people and books
Useful Addresses 211
Index 215

ON A PERSONAL NOTE

In my work as a journalist and writer as well as in my personal and everyday life, I have always been fascinated by the way in which some people managed to achieve their aims and ambitions while others seemed to spend their lives chasing their dreams. For my own part, I felt I had achieved many of the things I once only dreamed of. As a child I longed to be a writer. Later I lost sight of my ambition when I grew up, got married and had my two children (something else I wanted to do). My then partner and I dreamed of moving out of the city, growing our own fruit and vegetables, and bringing up our children in the peace and tranquillity of the countryside. We found a ramshackle country cottage and did just that. It was then that my original dream reasserted itself. One evening, after the goats had been milked and the children were tucked up in bed, I wrote two articles on the kitchen table – by candlelight (our idyllic cottage didn't have electricity!). I sent them off and to my delight they were accepted. I was on my way. At the same time I enrolled for another degree with the Open University, started a teaching course and began teaching sociology and psychology at my local college of further education. Sadly, my marriage wasn't to survive, so I bought a house in town nearby (another achievement) and within a year I had written my first book and was making a full-time living from journalism. Six years after this my life changed yet again. After years of living in the 'sticks' I missed the buzz and vitality of city life, so I uprooted to London, where I now live. I realised the delights of foreign travel somewhat late in life but now the desire to travel is one of my biggest 'wants' – my latest passion. Some of these things at the time appeared to happen more by luck than judgement. However, as I wrote this book I began to understand that, without always realising it, I had aimed myself in the direction I wanted to go, and that my way of approaching things I wanted to do actually conformed to a plan. I hope the insights that I have gained through my own personal experiences and through writing, researching and teaching will help you to gain what you want in life. Good luck to you – and enjoy the journey!

PART ONE
THE BASIC PLAN

INTRODUCTION

How often have you asked yourself, 'What will make me happy? What do I really want from life? Which way should I go?' And how often have you answered, 'I don't much care . . .' or, 'I don't know.' In a rapidly changing world, many of the certainties that guided the lives of our parents and grandparents have vanished. As a result many of us feel cut adrift, lacking direction and motivation. This is a pity, because there are more opportunities available today than ever before. However, if you don't know where you want to get to, how can you start to get there? It's only by having some idea of what you want that you will be in a position to recognise and pursue the opportunities that lie all around you.

One of the problems about getting what we want is that many of us feel guilty for wanting anything at all. We feel that wanting is greedy or selfish. As children we are often told, 'He who wants doesn't get,' or, 'You can't always have what you want.' When such messages are repeated over and over again, our wants get blurred by rules and injunctions laid down by other people – parents, teachers, employers and others. The result? We bury our desires and they remain unsatisfied.

There was a time when each one of us knew what we wanted. As newborn babies crying for the breast we had no doubts about our wants. As toddlers and small children we had a healthy sense of our own desires – as anyone who has witnessed a two-year-old temper tantrum knows! So the instinct for wanting is there but it may have become obscured. We can't seem to put our finger on exactly what we do want. We are aware of something missing, but we don't know what it is.

At first, it may be a nagging sense of dissatisfaction with our lives, a vague feeling of being stuck or that something is not quite right. If we ignore this feeling it can whip up to a raging storm of discontent. Sometimes such feelings are provoked by a major crisis of some kind: a crumbling marriage, redundancy, divorce or bereavement. But more often than not, it is simply the feeling that we could be getting more out of life.

Manufacturers and advertisers are only too happy to tap into our dissatisfaction and assuage our desires – at least temporarily. 'Shoes to die for,' screeches the headline at the beginning of the fashion section of a women's magazine. 'This season's "Must haves",' orders the style editor of another. We ourselves often attempt a quick fix for our discontent: 'Perhaps things will change if we have a baby,' you think as you attempt to come up with ways to rescue a relationship that appears to have lost its way. 'I'll meet the woman of my dreams when I start going to the gym,' you promise yourself. 'What you need is a holiday,' says a friend when you complain that you find your job boring. But, ultimately, that new pair of shoes, that exotic holiday, will only satisfy for a brief period, if they weren't really what we wanted. Once the euphoria of the new possession or experience has worn off, the sense of something missing creeps back. Deferred gratification, not getting what you want straightaway, is not always a bad thing. Unfortunately, however, we sometimes put our own needs and wants to one side for so long that we never actually achieve them.

This book, then, is all about wanting. It's about tapping into your deepest desires and coming up with answers to the questions:

- What sort of job do I want?
- What sort of partner do I want?
- What sort of life do I want?

It's not calculating, selfish or unspontaneous to consider these matters. In fact, whether you are aware of it or not, you *chose* to be where you are today. You may think you just arrived there, but even *not* making a choice – for example staying put in a relationship you know is not working, delaying applying for that promotion, vowing to start that diet tomorrow, and tomorrow . . . and tomorrow – are choices. The trouble is they aren't *powerful* choices. The result is that you drift through life rather than progressing purposefully towards your dreams. How much better to take some time to work out exactly what you want out of life and set about getting it with full awareness of where you are going. That way, you have some control over the direction in which your life is going and will be more likely to get the results *you* are looking for rather than those imposed by someone else.

In *How To Get What You Want* you will discover how to do all this. In Part One, you will learn how to identify your needs, desires and dreams, how to put those dreams into action, how to create the resources – money, time, skills and so on – to get what you want, and how to overcome problems and setbacks. In Part Two, you will find out how to get what you want in five areas of your life: your work, your relationships, your appearance, your health and your personal development. Finally, you will learn what to do if you don't get what you want, how to redraw your plans and look to the future. In Part Three, you will find stories of people who have got what they wanted, to cheer and inspire you. Throughout the book you will find quizzes, checklists and exercises to keep you on track and help you achieve what you desire. I suggest you buy a big notebook to do the various written exercises in. You will also need some sheets of paper. But, now, to give you a taste of what's to come, tick any of the following statements that apply to you:

- [ ] I don't know what I want
- [ ] I want to find out who I am
- [ ] I know what I want but I don't know how to get it
- [ ] I feel I'm in a rut
- [ ] I'd like to change my life
- [ ] I find it difficult to make choices about what I want to do
- [ ] I don't know where to go from here

Did you tick any of them? If so, then you are reading the right book. Let's get started.

CHAPTER ONE
DEFINING WHAT YOU WANT

Perhaps the biggest problem most of us face when thinking about what we want is quite simply deciding what it is. I can remember numerous occasions sitting with friends in wine bars when the conversation has drifted to what we want out of life and I have heard the phrase, 'I don't want to go on doing this for the rest of my life – but I don't know what else to do.' One of the problems, as we shall see later in this book, is that our brains find it hard to deal with negatives – things we don't want to do. A negative desire creates a black hole in your brain. A positive desire creates a spark: you find yourself thinking 'Aah,' or 'What if?', and from there it's a question of following your imagination. The secret of discovering what you want is that there is no secret. The knowledge is already there inside you. It's simply a matter of freeing your brain to develop the insights and make the connections necessary to bring this knowledge into the light of day. And the key that unlocks the door is something you possess already: your own imagination.

In the world we live in today, most of the activities of our everyday lives require us to be logical and cool-headed, to think things through step by step. These are all operations that use the left side of our brains. Using our imagination, on the other hand, is a right-brain activity: it involves intuition rather than logic, pictures rather than words, making connections between unlikely partners rather than moving in a straight line from A to B. It is the world of the possible – and the impossible. In this chapter, you will learn how you can tap into your imagination and use it to guide you in defining what you want. But first look at three questions that are crucial to getting what you want:

- Who am I?
- Where have I come from?
- Where am I going?

The rest of this chapter is devoted to looking at these questions, using your imagination of course. Once you have answered them you will be ready for another set of questions, which we will look at over the following chapters. These include:

- How will I get there?
- Who will help me?
- What is stopping me?
- What will I be like when I get there?

So now you know what questions need answering, let's have a look at them each in turn.

WHO AM I?

One of the most inspiring books I have read on making changes is an autobiography by Joanna Field (Marion Milner) called *A Life of One's Own*, originally published in 1934. In it she writes:

> *If my life was not satisfactory as it was, in what way was I to change it? By what standard was I to guide it?*
>
> *Here I began to consider by what standards I had been guiding it. If I could find that out then I might know what to avoid in the future. Here, though I did not guess it at the time, was a most important step, for*

> instead of trying to force myself into doing what I imagined I ought to do I began to enquire what I was doing. I little knew what this apparently simple act of trying to be aware of my own experience would involve me in.
>
> My first attempt was a consideration of all the things that I seemed to be aiming at . . . being good at one's job, pleasing people, being popular, not missing things, doing what's expected of one, not letting people down, helping people, being happy. As soon as I began to think about it I saw that whichever of these aims might be the most important to work for I would not achieve it; for my life was determined, not by any one of them, but by a planless mixture of them all. I discovered that I was drifting without rudder or compass, swept in all directions by influence from custom, tradition, fashion, swayed by standards uncritically accepted from my friends, my family, my countrymen, my ancestors.
>
> I decided to look at the facts of my own life, to see if I could find out what I wanted to know simply by observation and experiment. I thought that I would try to observe what my wants were and whether I got them and whether it made me happy or not.

For Milner, the key to happiness was, as the ancient Greek oracle at Delphi put it, 'Know yourself.' Self-knowledge is still one of the keys to getting what you want. Knowing yourself gives you the power to direct your life in the way you want, because it enables you to harness your own strengths and motivation and find ways of overcoming your weaknesses. You can observe the person you are and experiment with what you do so as to create the life you want to live. The first step is to look at who you are.

FINDING OUT ABOUT YOU

To read some of the newspapers you would think that we are all endowed with a fixed personality. The tabloids love simple labels: 'Fun-loving Fergie', the Duchess of York; 'Shy Di', the Princess of Wales; the 'Iron Lady', Margaret Thatcher. Yet such stereotypes tell us little about real people. You only have to compare yourself with a friend to be aware of your uniqueness and the many ways you have of expressing your individual identity. The way you dress, the house you live in, your possessions, the car you drive, the lifestyle you choose to live, all express something about you and the way you want to be seen by the world.

The question 'Who am I?' can be answered in many ways: you could give your name, your gender, your nationality, your roles as mother, brother, friend, boss, employee, or you could explain something about your beliefs, ideals, worries, interests or ambitions. All these factors, but especially your knowledge of this deeper 'you', are important when considering what you want. So now let's take a look at you, who you are, your strengths and your weaknesses.

THINKING ABOUT WHO YOU ARE

To do this you need some time on your own free from distractions, and a pen and notebook.

> Using a page of the notebook describe who you are. You can do it in any way you like – by writing it down, by drawing a picture of yourself (it doesn't have to be a work of art; a 'stick' figure will do), by drawing a tree with the branches each representing an aspect of you. It doesn't matter how you choose to represent yourself – just use your imagination. Use the following suggestions as prompts:
>
> - Your body: what do you like about it (dark hair, soft skin, long legs – we've all got some good points!)? What things are you less keen on (doughy stomach, hairy chest, skinny arms)? What about your health (good eyesight, strong teeth, healthy heart)?
>
> - Your mind: how does it tick (logical, imaginative, perceptive, intuitive, mathematical)? What gives you pleasure about the way your mind works? What would you like to improve (better at maths, more logical)?
>
> - Your emotions: what are your primary feelings (fear, anger, enthusiasm, joy)? What things give you most pleasure and what the most pain?

- **Your achievements:** what things have you done that you are proud of (giving birth, your job, becoming a youth club leader)?
- **Your skills:** what are your skills (are you good with words, with people, with things, with ideas)?
- **Your likes and dislikes:** think about your favourite/least favourite things (place, time of year, time of day, colour, book, music, car, food, clothes). Consider the things you do for enjoyment (watching TV, walking in the countryside, listening to Mozart) – and those you would go to the end of the earth to avoid (writing to the bank manager, emptying the dustbin, anything to do with maths).

What have you found out about yourself? You are already beginning to discover and appreciate yourself as a unique and precious individual.

WHERE HAVE I COME FROM?

Who you are, of course, is more than simply a matter of chance. The place you were born, where you were brought up, the schools you went to, your parents, your friends, your religion or lack of it – all these things have shaped your personal history. Even if your background was superficially the same as a friend or relative, the details of your experience make it unique. For example, if you felt sure of your parents' love and affection, you are likely to be secure and confident in your dealings with other people. On the other hand, if you were deprived of affection as a child, you may grow up to be insecure, expect rejection, and perhaps seek out love from impossible people.

Now it's time to delve a little more deeply into who you are by looking at where you have come from. You will need some time and a pen and notebook.

Using a page in your notebook, write and fill in the following:

- **1. People in my life**

My parents were ....

My childhood heroes were ....

The people I most disliked as a child were ....

Important people in my life in the past were ....

- 2. **Places in my life**

I was born ....

I was brought up ....

I went to school at ....

- 3. **Happenings in my life**

Major events in my life were ....

Painful experiences in my life were ....

Formative experiences in my life were ....

- 4. **My beliefs**

My childhood dreams and ambitions were ....

My parents' ambitions for me were ....

As a child I was brought up to believe ....

My religion was/is ....

How did you get on? Doing this exercise will have revealed the various experiences and people that have influenced who you are. Were there any surprises? Did you discover things about yourself that you didn't know, had forgotten or failed to recognise?

LOOKING AT YOUR PERSONALITY

So, all sorts of things go to make up who you are: the genetic blueprint you have inherited from your parents, what you have learned from other people and your experiences of life. Psychologists often distinguish between traits – stable aspects of our personalities – and states – passing moods. For example, if you are shy in every situation your shyness would be described as a trait. On the other hand, if you are only shy in certain situations, for example if you have to meet a famous person, your shyness would be described as a state. Many traits are, like aspects of our physical appearance, part of our genetic blueprint.

One of the most exciting discoveries psychologists have made is that we ourselves are active in shaping who we are. For example, if you are shy and go out to dinner with friends you may sit and listen quietly and do nothing to join in. If you are sociable, you will look for gaps in the chat and try to find a way to enter the conversation. The person with exhibitionist tendencies will act the fool or find some other way to grab all the attention. Behaving in this way tends to reinforce characteristics such as shyness or sociability.

At the same time, you may choose to put yourself into situations where you can express particular parts of your personality that you like. Given the choice of going to a party or a library, sociable individuals will choose the party and once there will do their best to display their sociability by moving from group to group, talking to lots of people and so on. Even if they have to go to the library, they will seek out ways of expressing their sociability, perhaps chatting to the person in the queue for the photocopier. Of course, none of us is purely one thing or another: most of us adapt to the situations we find ourselves in, so a cocktail party may bring out your sociable, gregarious side; a conference, the intellectual, academic side.

YOU CAN CHANGE WHO YOU ARE

These psychological insights are of more than academic interest because now you know about them, you can begin to use them to change yourself and become the person you want to be. One of the simplest ways is to change the way you act and see how this changes the way others react to you. For example, if you are shy you can choose to expose yourself to social situations and so learn ways of coping with or conquering your shyness so it doesn't cripple you in your dealings with other people.

FINDING YOUR NICHE

When it comes to getting what you want – and feeling happy – it's all a question of finding the right niche. If you thrive on a fast pace of life, a job in the money markets with their frantic buying and selling is likely to suit you; the quiet life of a gardener would probably drive you up the wall. The same goes for finding a partner. If you are a life and soul of the party type who likes to be out dancing every night of the week, you are unlikely to be happy with someone who prefers to spend their time pottering around the house or reading the newspaper.

If your situation doesn't suit your personality – if you are a round peg in a square hole – you have several options. You can accept the situation and try to express your personality in other ways. If you are an extremely active person but your job involves sitting down in front of a computer all day, you may become even keener to seek out energetic pursuits in your spare time. On the other hand, you can choose to place less importance on that aspect of your personality. For example, if you are extremely sociable but forced to go and live on a desert island for a few years, you may become so used to isolation that you no longer mind it. Or your desire to mix with others may become so strong that you will do almost anything to get off that island. However, it's probably true to say that if you feel like a round peg in a square hole in any area of your life, you are likely to experience severe strain – unless you can find some other outlet for the aspect of your personality that is denied.

THIS IS YOUR LIFE

In the rest of this chapter, you will learn how to start thinking about the direction in which you want to go. But let's just tie up what you have found out about who you are and where you have come from. The aim of the following exercise is to highlight any unfinished business which may be hampering you today, so freeing you to concentrate on getting what you want in the future. It sometimes helps to do the exercise with a friend. You will need some time, a felt-tipped pen and a large piece of paper.

1. Take the piece of paper and draw a line on it. This represents your lifeline. Draw it in any way that makes sense to you: a straight line, or one with peaks and troughs. You could even draw a big picture of the palm of your hand and draw the line on that.

2. Now mark the line to show where you are today.

3. Now write in or draw the main events in your life that have influenced who you are today. Go back as far as you remember and continue up to the present.

4. As you write down or draw the significant events in your life, try to evoke the detail of each experience. Think about what you were wearing, what other people were wearing, what the weather was like, what you said, what they said, how you felt. Take your time and be as specific as possible.

5. Now consider the following questions:

- What does your lifeline say about the way you have lived your life and the beliefs you now hold? Think about the feelings and thoughts you have developed in response to various events. For example: Mum's depression when I left home to go to college (event) has left me with a fear (feeling) of being independent. That's why I always tend to pick partners who I lean on (thought); Dad's way of retreating behind the paper every time a discussion about feelings was on the cards (event) left me with a fear (feeling) of showing my emotions. In fact, deep down I believe that showing emotions is wrong (thought); the algebra teacher making me go up to the front of the class and do an equation on the board in front of the whole class (event) has made me lack confidence (feeling) about dealing with figures. That's why I am hopeless at anything mathematical (thought).

- What elements are needed for you to consider an event to be a high spot? What things are important to you (your feelings, financial success or recognition, having people close to you present)?

- What were the most important beliefs you developed from the high spots in your life? 'I am good at passing exams', 'I am strong', 'Good things are a matter of luck', 'I'm a winner', 'I can do what I want to do'?

- What were the most important beliefs you developed from the low spots in your life? 'I can't cope', 'I'm not successful at managing relationships', 'I am strong', 'I will survive'?

Following this exercise will enable you to see where some of your beliefs about yourself have come from. You will also begin to see how your views are helping or hindering you at present. This will enable you to be more in charge of what happens now. At the same time you are developing a clearer idea of who you are so you can start the exciting process of directing your life in the way you want it to go in the future.

Remember: the way you react doesn't have to be set in stone. What has happened has happened, you can't change that, but you can change how you respond and how you interpret events. You'll see later on in the book how people who have an upbeat, optimistic approach to life tend to be better at getting what they want. And you will learn how you can transform your negative thoughts into positive ones.

Just before we leave who you are and where you come from, think about two more questions: are you a risk-taker or do you go for the safe option? If you do take risks do they usually turn out well or badly?

WHERE AM I GOING?

So here you are, a unique individual with your own physical appearance, your own experiences of life, your own relatives and friends, your own beliefs, feelings, dreams and ambitions. How do you start to get where you want to go? The first step is to look at where you are going now.

- 'Would you tell me, please, which way I ought to go from here?'
  'That depends a good deal on where you want to get to,' said the cat.
  'I don't much care where . . .' said Alice.
  'Then it doesn't matter which way you go,' said the cat.
  Alice in Wonderland, Lewis Carroll

If you don't know where you want to get to then, like Alice, you risk setting off in all directions at once, trying to split yourself in too many different parts, or being so confused that you never set out at all.

BRAINSTORMING

To help you find out where you are going – an essential exercise in deciding where you want to go – let me introduce you to a technique known as brainstorming. You will need some time and a pen and notebook.

> 1. In the middle of a page write: 'Where am I going?'
>
> 2. Write down as many things that inspire you and give you energy as you can. Don't censor your thoughts, write down what springs to mind. Consider: your childhood dreams, your present dreams and fantasies, your qualities, talents, enthusiasms, opportunities, inspirations such as fairy stories or biographies of famous people.
>
> 3. Now make connections between the various strands – join them up and think about their implications. For example: how does your fantasy of going to live on a Greek island relate to your favourite fairy tale of *Jack and the Beanstalk*? How does it relate to your enthusiasm for photography? Can you begin to see any themes, patterns and directions emerging?

Doing this exercise will have enabled you to start thinking about the direction you are headed in now and whether it is really where you want to go. You may already be beginning to find some new directions – if so, write them down in your notebook. As you read on through the book you will learn how to use your fantasies to guide you, how to make a plan of action and how to set goals so you get to where you want to go, rather than just drifting. But before we go on, there is another way of tapping into the power of your imagination.

VISUALISING YOUR POSSIBLE SELVES

This is another very simple technique to get in touch with what you want. It's called visualisation, or guided imagination, and in effect it is a sophisticated form of daydreaming. Visualisation is an extremely powerful way of tapping into your deepest needs and desires. As children we all tend to daydream – to lose ourselves in the world of our imagination. But as we get older, many of us lose the ability to roam the world of our unconscious minds. This is a pity because they are in touch with our deepest needs. How often have you slept on a problem and come up with the solution the next day?

To examine how visualisation might work think about this: our lives are a bit like a play or film script in which each one of us is the hero or heroine. Whenever we encounter a new experience or situation – a new scene in the script – we try out how we are going to deal with it by focusing on an imaginary mental scenario. We then try to decide how to play this particular scene, drawing partly on our knowledge of ourselves and how we have acted in similar situations in the past. We also project ourselves into the future and imagine how we might play it. Psychologists call this creature of our imaginations our 'possible self'.

Your possible self reflects your goals, aspirations, beliefs and fears. He or she is the person you think you *could* become, would *like* to become, or *fear* becoming. The range of roles each of us can choose from is enormous. The person you would like to be may be the successful, accomplished businessman or woman, the witty, creative artist, the warm, loving friend, the admired pillar of the community. At the other end of the spectrum is the self you dread – the 'bag lady', the tiresome bore who everyone avoids at a party, the fat, ugly person who never does anything right. Possible roles also include those specified by important people in your present or past: your parents, teachers, friends, partners. The person you are allowed (or not allowed) to be or to become: 'You ought to train to be a doctor, like your father.' 'You can't go to Cambridge, everyone else in our family went to Oxford.'

Your own particular cast of characters is highly individual. Even though we may have the same goal, what it means to each of us will vary. The abstract goal of 'getting a degree', say, will be transformed in your imagination into what this means for you. Your possible self – your image of yourself with a degree – may include having a new job, a new car, a nice flat, new friends, gaining the admiration of your parents and friends, even looking more attractive. Visualisation involves consciously tapping into your personal movie, imagining your possible selves and then consciously choosing the one you want to be.

To prove to yourself that visualisation works, try this exercise.

1. Take your notebook and write down at the top of three pages: 'My dream job', 'My dream day', 'My dream life'.

2. Now think about each of them in turn and imagine what it would involve. Take your time and really get into each dream. Use the following prompts to make up your own list, and add any others that are important for you:

Dream job

- How much do you earn?
- What does the job involve?
- Who do you work with?
- What does your working day/week involve?
- What sort of lifestyle goes with the job?
- Where are you living – in this country or abroad?
- Are you living in a house or a flat?

- Where do you eat; restaurants, the works canteen, at home?

- Add anything else you can think of ....

Dream day

- Will you be outside or inside? The weather, the furnishings?

- What you are wearing?

- The smells? The colours? Would anyone be there with you? What time would your day start?

Dream life

- How long do you want to live?

- What job/career would you have?

- What sort of lifestyle would you pursue?

- Who would you have around you?

3. Now focus on each one in turn: the people with you, the place you are in, the smell of the air, the cooling breeze. The more detailed picture you can build up, the more effective your imaginary scenario will be in helping you access your deepest desires. Don't censor your imagination. The whole point is to give it free rein.

Now you are ready to analyse what this exercise tells you about your wants, needs and desires. For example, if your day involved a dinner party in the Italian villa you bought (remember we're talking imagination here) with your children, your lover, your father, who is dead, write it down. Your imaginary scenario gives you clues about your innermost needs. For example, your father's presence may indicate something missing from your life: is it someone 'wise' to talk problems over with? Or simply that you never get a chance to talk to anyone about your passion for literature? If so, could those needs be satisfied by cultivating an older friend, deciding to see a counsellor, or enrolling on an evening course in literature?

Think about what you have found out about what you want. Which aspects of you are being satisfied in your present life? Which aspects are being denied? Which ones do you need to think about changing? What have you learned about yourself and what is important to you? Can you bring this knowledge to bear on the decisions you make about your life? Are any elements of your dreams achievable now? Could any of them be achievable in the future? How can you achieve some of what you dream about in your life? What might stand in the way of you achieving some of your dreams? How might you get round them? What aims do you want to set yourself as a result of doing this visualisation?

DEFINING WHAT YOU WANT ROUND UP

You are now ready to explore yourself even more deeply, to probe the things that make you tick, that give you energy and inspire you. But first have a look at the following statements:

- ☐ I recognise and appreciate myself as a unique individual.
- ☐ I know where I am coming from and the influences that have made me who I am.
- ☐ I can tap into my dreams and focus on the things that are important to me.
- ☐ I can imagine myself growing more confident as I learn more about who I am and what I want.

Now you're ready for the next step, finding the motivation to get going.

CHAPTER TWO
GETTING GOING

YOU CAN DO IT

Getting what you want isn't always difficult once you know how. We've already looked at ways to identify some of the things you want. In the next chapter you'll see what you can do to turn those dreams into reality, but first let's have a look at what will fuel your determination to get what you desire. You may imagine that the most important factor in getting what you want is willpower. Well, there you are wrong! In fact the secret is motivation. Motivation is what gives you the energy to start and keeps you going when you encounter setbacks.

If you find it hard to distinguish between motivation and willpower, consider someone who is learning to play the guitar, perhaps as part of his dream to become a famous rock star. At first the novelty and excitement of having an instrument and learning to play it are enough. But sooner or later, if he is to achieve his dream, he must face up to the hard slog of practice. That might mean missing other things he enjoys, like listening to his CDs, going out with his friends, or watching TV. No amount of willpower, however rigorously applied, will carry him through unless he also has the motivation. The same principle applies in every single area of life, from forming a relationship to running a business. Motivation means wanting to take control of your life rather than drifting through it. It's motivation that gives you the confidence to resolve, 'Yes, I want to . . . and I am going to.' To harness your motivation, you have to examine your life honestly and understand yourself so you have the conviction that allows you to take control.

ENHANCING YOUR MOTIVATION

The feeling that you *should* or *ought* to do something is not as powerful a motivator as wanting or needing to do it. True, *should* and *ought* messages are often very strong indeed. This is because they often derive from people in authority, such as our parents, teachers, religious leader or boss. To get the motivation to start getting what you want, however, it's *your* wants and needs that count.

> Motivation means thinking about the following:
> - Why you want to make a particular change
> - What the change is for
> - Who you are doing it for
> - What benefits you will gain from it

MAKING CHOICES

At the end of the day getting what you want means weighing up the gains you will make from a particular choice against any losses. To be successful in pursuing your goals your desire to go for them must be greater than your desire to stay the same. One simple method of finding out what you stand to gain from pursuing anything you want is to do what the experts call a cost-benefit analysis, a sort of balance sheet of pros and cons. Let's see how it works in practice. You will need some time and a pen and notebook.

> 1. Think about one of the things you want to do in any of the key areas of your life and write it down at the top of the page. On one side of the page write down 'Costs' and on the other write down 'Benefits'.

> 2. Now list all the pros and cons you can think of if you were to pursue the goal you are thinking about under the appropriate heading. The costs and benefits can be financial, physical, emotional, practical – anything that you feel is important in weighing up your decision.
>
> 3. Now rate each cost and benefit on a scale of one to five according to how you feel. If you feel one of the costs is a very high price to pay, rate it as five. Now circle the two highest costs and the two most attractive benefits of pursuing that particular course.

Once you have done this you have some data on which to base your choice. It's now simply a matter of working out whether the costs of your chosen course are outweighed by the benefits, and if not what you can do to reduce the costs, or increase the benefits. You can use this method every time you have a choice to make; if you have several different choices to make, you can work out the one that offers you the most.

So now let's look at some of the things you might want and why they are important.

MORE ABOUT WHAT YOU WANT AND HOW TO GET IT

Our main desires revolve around a set of needs that is shared by all human beings. Whether you are a starving peasant in Africa or a high-flying executive, you have certain basic bodily needs that ensure your survival. These include the need for food, sleep, water, warmth and comfort. You also have the need for safety and security, for protection from danger, violence, and other outside threats.

Over and above these basic physical needs, there are emotional and spiritual needs. We all need to feel that we belong and are accepted by our family, friends, partner and those around us. We also need to feel we are recognised and approved of, that our skills and talents are appreciated and valued by other people. Last, but not least, we need to fulfil our natural creativity and potential and to feel that our lives have a sense of purpose and meaning.

It is only once our basic survival needs have been met that we can be free to concentrate on other needs. If you have to beg for your food, all your energies are concentrated on basic survival; there's little energy left for fulfilling your creativity. Similarly, if you have just been made redundant you are likely to be less concerned with the meaning of life than making sure your mortgage is paid. Some psychologists have defined four basic psychological needs. These are:

- The need for love
- The need for freedom of choice
- The need to have fun
- The need to feel a degree of control and power over your own life

Your precise goals will depend on you as an individual, and so will the means you use to achieve them. For example one person who wants a trimmer figure might choose to go on a diet, another might enrol at a gym, while a third might have the fat sucked from their thighs by liposuction. We'll be looking at some of the options in more detail in Part Two of this book. But what you want will probably fall into one of several well-defined categories, which you'll notice echo those basic needs. They include:

- Career and work
- Sex and relationships
- Appearance
- Long life and health
- Personal growth and development

We're now going to look at each one of these in turn, together with a few of the motivators in each category. At the end you will have the opportunity to think about what you want in this category and write down the benefits you would gain if you were to get it. This will provide you with a list of motivating factors that are unique to you.

Don't feel you have to fill in each category – some may be more personally relevant to you than others. It all depends on your basic values and beliefs. However, the act of writing down what you want is important, because it makes it concrete. What you note down is the first step in developing your own personal blueprint for getting what you want. It's also the first stage of your promise to yourself. Let's get started.

CAREER AND WORK

Finding satisfying work or a career is high on most people's agenda, for the simple reason that doing work you enjoy is an important part of who you are (think back to the 'Who am I?' exercise). Work helps us to obtain social recognition, approval, and respect – one of the basic needs. It also contributes to our self-esteem and self-respect, helps us structure our time and helps us make sense of the world – in other words, it helps give our lives meaning. A job also satisfies our need for contact with other people (think for a moment about how many of your friends and acquaintances are people you have met at work – you'll probably be surprised). And of course work also brings in the wherewithal to buy some of the material things we want.

> Think about what you want to do to develop your career, visualise what benefits you would gain and write them down. Be very specific and detailed, for example: a salary of . . . . . . per year. The more vividly you can visualise your gains, the more powerful your motivation.
>
> - I want to develop my career in the following way . . . .
> - I want to change my job to . . . .
> - I want to develop the following skills in my job . . . .

- I want to gain the following qualifications ....
- The gains I visualise getting from this are ....

SEX AND RELATIONSHIPS

Close friendships, sexual intimacy, companionship and the love and support of friends and family figure highly on most people's 'I want' list. This is not surprising, since intimate relationships are vital to our need for mental and physical health and self-esteem. Research has shown that people who are married or co-habiting are less likely to suffer from depression, cancer and heart disease. Not surprisingly, the loss of a spouse or sexual partner is one of the most devastating and stressful life events. Research into happiness shows that people who are happily married are more satisfied with life overall. In fact, social psychologist Michael Argyle sums it up well when he says, 'To enhance happiness one should get married, stay married, have children, keep up with relatives, have plenty of friends, and keep on good terms with the neighbours.' For "married" you can also substitute having an intimate relationship with one person.

Write down what you want in the area of sex and relationships and visualise the gains you would get from them. Don't forget – be specific. Think about whether you want to marry, have children, which people you want to have as friends, which relatives you want around you and any other desires relating to other people.

- In the area of relationships I want the following..........
- The benefits I visualise gaining from this are...............

APPEARANCE

Like it or not the way you look is important – witness the millions of diet and exercise manuals. Research shows that – at least on first acquaintance

– we are judged by what we look like. All of us make rapid – usually quite unconscious – judgements of people we meet within a few minutes of encountering them. Psychologists surmise that the reason we do this is to maintain our sense of control over the world. Research also shows that we equate facial features such as thin lips with meanness, thick lips with sensuality, and people who wear glasses with intellect. We tend to endow people we consider to be good-looking with all sorts of desirable mental and social qualities too. Studies have proved that people who are deemed attractive are also judged to be more sociable, dominant, sexier, mentally stable, intelligent and socially skilled; we don't always consider them to be more honest, genuine, sincere, trustworthy, moral or kind! So looking good relates to our basic need for approval, liking and self-esteem. Given these facts, it's hardly surprising that appearance comes high on most people's list of 'wants'.

> Write down what you want to change (if anything) in your appearance as well as the benefits you would gain from making such changes. Think about your weight, height, hair, skin, clothing and all aspects of the way you look. And don't forget – be specific.
>
> • The way I want to look is..
> • The benefits I would gain from this are........................

LONG LIFE AND HEALTH

Given the choice, most of us would opt for a long and healthy life so we can enjoy what we have worked for. Good health enables us to do many of the things we want to do – and so to satisfy our basic needs on many different levels. Research has shown that longevity is closely linked to our genes. But even if you haven't been blessed with long-lived parents, there are plenty of things you can do to keep yourself healthy so you can enjoy your life – however long it turns out to be. These include eating a healthy diet, making sure you get enough exercise, making time for rest and relaxation, and giving up harmful habits like smoking or drinking to excess.

> Think about what you want in the way of health; include any health problems you want to sort out such as giving up smoking, drinking to excess and other unhealthy habits, and include any changes you want to make in your diet, exercise, rest and relaxation. Then write down the benefits you would gain from this.
>
> - I want the following for my health..............................
> - The benefits I visualise gaining are..............................

PERSONAL GROWTH AND DEVELOPMENT

Personal growth and development, or self-actualisation as some psychologists call it, is perhaps the one thing that all of us are striving for. It's about fulfilling ourselves in every area of our lives and feeling more whole, rounded people. It can include being creative in a particular field of art, music or science or simply applying creativity in the way we think about life and try to solve problems. It usually includes searching for a personal meaning in your own life, whether by means of an organised religion, something like New Age philosophy, or simply by finding your own code of values and beliefs which guides you in what you do. Above all, it means using your full potential and being in charge of your own life and destiny. Your wants in this area may be less easy to define, but are none the less important. In fact, they are probably the most important of all.

> Think about what you want for yourself and how you would like to grow and the benefits you would gain from it.
>
> - I want to grow in the following ways ....
> - The benefits I would gain are ....

A WORD ABOUT MONEY

You may wonder why I haven't listed money as one of the things we all want. After all, you may well imagine that you have no problems that winning a lottery wouldn't solve. Indeed, one of the first books on getting what you want, *How to get what you want out of life*, originally written in 1957 by US career and business consultant William J. Reilly, lists money as one of 'the four things everybody wants'. I disagree. Of course, money may be one of your motivators. It can also help you to get some of the things you want and put your plans into action (you'll find out all about how you can create it in Chapter 5). However, research has shown that money doesn't actually make us happier. True, some psychologists have found that rich people are a little more content and satisfied with life in general, but only by a small margin. It appears that once we've got the basics, having more money doesn't actually make us any more satisfied with our lives, nice though it is to be able to afford a new car, designer clothes, exotic holidays and so on. In fact, people who have won large sums of money often find they are actually less contented than before – often because they have given up their jobs and lost touch with family, friends and many of the other aspects of life that provide them with satisfaction and a sense of identity.

What really seems to matter is what money means for you. Wealth for some people is a mark of success and this in turn may boost their self-esteem. However, for many people success and money aren't linked. You can be earning a decent salary, in a secure job, in a firm you like, and yet still feel that something is missing in your life. The missing factor is likely to be to do with feeling that you are fulfilling your true potential, being creative and in charge of your own life – which of course brings us back to personal growth and fulfilment.

INSPIRATIONS

One of the biggest motivators is other people's example: we all need encouragement as we make changes in our lives, something or someone to keep us going towards the finishing line when the going gets tough. I call these people inspirations. We all have people we admire both now and in the past. They can be: a good friend, teachers, public figures, famous sports people, film stars, historical figures, or anyone who has achieved something. Your inspiration doesn't have to be someone who has achieved in the area you want to change; it can be someone whose philosophy and beliefs you admire and find encouraging. For example, when I was trying to persuade my doctor to let me give birth to my second daughter at home I drew much encouragement from a mountaineer who I heard talking on the radio about the nature of risk. He said, 'If you aren't prepared to take some risks in life you'll never do anything that is worth doing. You might as well not have lived.' That thought provided me with the courage and strength to do all I could to reach my goal. And I did. Another inspiration for me was a fellow journalist, who I later got to know. When I was trying to make it as a struggling freelancer in the early days of my career I read her articles avidly and thought, 'If she can do it I can.'

If your inspiration is a famous figure, either past or present, try and track down things that have been written by or about him or her. Some ideas:

- Write down the qualities your inspiration had or developed which helped him or her to reach his or her goals and make a list of any wise or witty things your inspiration said.

- If your inspiration is someone you know, talk to that person about what you are planning to do.

- If your inspiration is no longer alive, think back to incidents which exhibited the qualities you are aiming for and write them down to encourage you.

- Allow your reflection on your inspiration's behaviour to fuel your progress towards your goals.

In Part Three of *How to Get What You Want* you'll find some inspirations to help motivate you.

GETTING GOING ROUND UP

Now you have found the things that motivate you, read the following statements and tick the ones that apply to you:

> ☐ I feel confident that I can identify the things that I want
> ☐ I feel confident that I can identify the things that motivate me
> ☐ I can identify the people who inspire me
> ☐ I am determined to get what I want

You are now ready to move on to the next step: turning your dreams into reality. You'll find out all about how in the next chapter.

CHAPTER THREE
TURNING YOUR DREAMS INTO REALITY

So now you have some ideas about what you want you are ready to embark on the most vital – and the most exciting – part of your campaign to change your life: turning your dreams into reality. Your dreams, as we have seen, are essential to provide the inspiration and the motivation to try for what you want. In this chapter, you will learn how to harness your imagination and energy to make those dreams come true. You will learn how to take control of your life, and how to make effective decisions and choices that will allow you to achieve what you desire.

Doing what you want means focusing on what you want to achieve, setting yourself goals, checking your progress and generally taking charge of your own life instead of just letting it happen. Bear in mind that any worthwhile change takes time, especially if you are lacking in self-confidence as you start to take control of your life. Rest assured that as you work through the various stages your confidence will improve as you start to see yourself achieving what you have set out to do. And along with your improved confidence and belief in yourself, your ability to control your life and get what you want will also increase.

The basic plan laid out here is the one that you will follow from now on whenever you want to achieve anything. It applies whatever your ambitions are and wherever they lie – whether they are in the worlds of friendship, family, work, money, leisure time, personal growth or anything else. It consists of five basic steps:

> Step one: Get in touch with your dream
>
> Step two: Research your dream
>
> Step three: Think out your plan of action
>
> Step four: Put your plan into action
>
> Step five: Check your progress

Simply by reading this far you have already taken the first step in getting in touch with your dream. This chapter is concerned with looking at the other four steps in a bit more detail so you can progress a little further along the road. So let's get started.

STEP 2: RESEARCHING YOUR DREAM

Information gathering is essential in starting to bring your dreams down to earth and making them real. You'll find more specific details about the sort of information you might look for in the various areas of your life and how to go about getting it in Part Two. What you will be looking for in most cases is not just pure information but applied or working knowledge. This means finding the facts, examining them and then thinking about how they might apply to you. What you learn will help you to take action. Some ways to build your working knowledge are:

- Scour books, newspapers, magazine articles and specialist publications for the subject you are investigating. Whatever you are trying to find out about there's bound to be a book about it, from personal relationships to how to work the Stock Exchange.
- Use the media. Keep your eye out for TV programmes, films, videos about the subject you are investigating. It's strange, but once you are focused on something you will find it popping up everywhere, a bit like the newly pregnant woman who suddenly starts to notice prams wherever she goes.

- Talk to other people. The people you talk to can be professionals – people in the business you are planning to enter if you are planning to change your career, for example – friends, relatives, even casual acquaintances. You'll probably be amazed at the knowledge you can pick up simply by talking to others about your dreams and ambitions, even people who you might not think know anything about the subject in question. Ask the person you are talking to if they know anyone else who might be able to help you, and write their names in your diary or contacts book.

The sort of information you will be looking for will vary, depending on the nature of your plan. It may involve looking back at the past and thinking about jobs you especially enjoyed doing, if you are trying to think of ways to develop your skills and talents in the area of your job. It may involve some lateral thinking too – bypassing the obvious solution for something more imaginative. One way to do this is to use the process of brainstorming, described in Chapter One. You will also need to do some research into hard facts such as:

- How much money is this likely to cost me?
- How much time will I need?
- Will I need to involve other people in my plans and if so who?

Information is rarely pure fact – it all depends on the angle you are coming from and the way you see things. So as you look, listen and learn, ask yourself the following questions:

- Who is giving me this information?
- Does this person have any particular axe to grind?
- What data, e.g. statistics, case histories, reports, are being used to back up this information?
- How does this information fit in with what I already know?
- How does what I have found out fit with my own experience?

STEP 3: THINKING OUT A PLAN OF ACTION

The next step in turning your dreams into reality is to make yourself a plan. The bigger the dream the bigger the plan, but every plan has to start somewhere and the way to start is to set yourself aims or goals.

Setting yourself goals is one of the most vital parts of getting what you want. If you don't have aims, you will only get where you want to be by accident – and it could take a long time. Setting goals speeds up the journey by showing you the direction in which you need to go, and enabling you to check your progress. This in turn enables you to go for your next goal. And so, step by step, you reach the sky.

STAYING FLEXIBLE

Our goals are rarely fixed: they change as we move through life and the circumstances of our lives change. Your aim at 18 might have been to pass your exams and enter university, at 22 it might have been to get a job in which you made £25,000 a year, at 32 with a partner and a child to support suddenly your goal is to earn £35,000 a year and to spend more time with your partner and child. It's important to keep an eye on your goals and check that they haven't changed while you weren't looking. The decision you make today might be different from the one you would have made five years ago and more different still from the one you might make five, ten, twenty years from now. If you are having problems deciding on your goals don't worry. It takes practice. You may need to make many decisions and try putting them into action in lots of different situations to discover who you are and what is important to you. The main thing is to take the step to set yourself aims and targets and to start seeing them through. It doesn't matter if you feel confused. Bear in mind that the only thing that is certain in life is the prospect of change and keep your goals flexible enough to allow you to adapt to the inevitable changes that will come with time.

To help you appreciate how your goals have changed do the following exercise:

> 1. Write down your goals as you remember them when you were 18.
>
> 2. Now write them down as if you were 28.
>
> 3. Now write them down as if you were 38.
>
> 4. Now write them down as if you were 48.
>
> 5. Now write them down as if you were retirement age
>
> Ask yourself the following:
>
> - What changes in goals can I observe? What do these changes tell me about my attitudes and beliefs?
>
> - What goals have stayed the same? What does this say about me?
>
> - What do my overall goals say about how I see my future?
>
> Check: Whenever you set yourself a goal ask: 'Is this in line with my overall goals now?'

SETTING GOALS

Every dream, however ambitious, has to start somewhere and that somewhere is with what is called a short-term goal. Short-term goals are the things you can achieve in a specified, relatively short period of time: the things you plan to do today, tomorrow, next week, next month, even within a few months. There are three rules you should apply when setting your goals that make it more likely that you will achieve them:

> 1. Make them positive
>
> 2. Make them specific
>
> 3. Make them active

Let's look at these in turn.

■ Goals should be positive

The reason for this is that our brains find it easier to deal with a positive action than a negative one. A positive action is one that involves you in choosing to *do* something rather than *not* to do it. Think about stopping smoking. One reason many people who try to give up cigarettes find it difficult is because all their energies are directed towards *not* doing something rather than using positive energy to do something. As you've already learnt, sheer willpower is less effective than *motivation* or positive desire. An alternative and often very effective approach to stopping smoking is to exercise choice about whether to smoke a particular cigarette. Smokers still carry a packet of cigarettes with them and instead of placing a restriction – 'No, I mustn't,' a step which involves a great deal of willpower – they give themselves a choice: 'Yes, I can – but I choose not to.' When they experience the desire for a cigarette they focus on the experience of smoking it: they conjure up in their imagination the smell, the taste, the feelings that smoking arouses, they then think of the positive benefits they will gain from not smoking – fresher breath and clothes, more money, lower risk of lung cancer – and *make a choice*. They may choose to do something else instead such as to have a cup of tea, read a book, talk to a friend on the telephone. Whatever they choose, it is a positive choice. Making an active choice in this way reinforces motivation and creates a feeling of success – and success, as we all know, breeds more success – which makes it easier the next time. You can apply the same principle to all the goals you set yourself.

■ Goals should be specific

Short-term goals need to spell out very clearly exactly what you need to do and how you will know when you have accomplished it. For example 'Lose some weight' is not a specific enough goal. How much weight do you want/need to lose? How will you measure how your weight loss programme is progressing? Being specific also applies to more complex goals. It's fairly simple to decide that you want to lose 10 lbs, but what if your ultimate goal is to be a successful journalist? This is where you need to use some of the groundwork you have already done on self-knowledge so you can define what the goal means for you. Success is too vague a term: it means different things to different people. What does successful mean for you? Which newspapers/magazines will you have to write for to consider yourself successful? How much money will you need to earn a year to consider yourself successful? What subjects do you want to write about? How will you know when you are successful? Where will you live, what sort of lifestyle will you have? With larger goals you will usually need to break them down into a set of subtasks in order of time or importance (more about this later). For example:

- This week – write/ring the features editor of *Vogue* offering her my article on X.
- Next week, if I haven't heard anything call to discuss the idea.
- The day after, if my idea isn't accepted, think about re-angling it and trying somewhere else – and so on.

Goals should be active

As we've already seen, it's much easier to be active: to do something rather than to sit back and wait for things to happen. So your goals should include a list of things you have to do. If you are thinking about a change of career, for example, your list of do's might include: finding out about training courses for your chosen career, developing the necessary skills, applying for a course, or making a list of companies that you would be interested in applying to. Write down your goals for each project you undertake and make sure each one contains an active verb (a 'doing' word). If it doesn't, get back to the drawing board and work on your goal until you can write down something you can *do*.

STRUCTURING YOUR GOALS

So now you have some idea of how to set yourself goals you need to structure them, to give them shape, and make them personal to you. To do this you need first to look at your personal assets. What are you bringing to the task(s) you have set yourself? What resources will you need, do you have or could you develop that can help or hinder you in the pursuit of your goals? Your resources may include practical skills and academic qualifications you gained in school. Just as importantly they can include your life skills, the things you have learnt simply by being you and getting where you are today: your body language, your physical appearance, your physical health and strength, your attitudes towards life.

Other assets you may need are time and money. How much time do you need to achieve this particular goal? Does what you have in mind demand money – if so, how much and where are you going to get it from? A bank loan? Savings?

Think about what 'people' resources you have and will need to help you achieve your goals. Who will support and help you – your partner, friends, children, bank manager, therapist? Think very carefully about each of these and the nature of the help and support each can offer. Then translate this into further goals. For example, if you are planning to do a course to gain further qualifications, who is going to look after the children on the one day a week you plan to do the course? How much time will the course take up? Think about homework and preparation time as well as the time spent attending the course. How much money will you need? Got the idea? OK, then it's time to move on to the next step, putting your plan into action, but first, check out your goals:

- Is the aim I have set myself positive? If not, think about ways in which you can turn it into something positive.

- Does the aim I have set myself represent *exactly* what I want?

- What do I have to do to achieve this aim?

- How will I know when I have achieved my aim? How can I measure my success in reaching this goal?

STEP 4: PUTTING YOUR PLAN INTO ACTION

Once you have worked out your goals, set yourself short-term and long-term goals and thought about what you need to do, it's time for action stations. Only you can put your plan into action but as you proceed with your plan enjoy the satisfaction of using all your skills. While you are performing each action concentrate totally on what you are doing. Learn to ignore extraneous factors. One technique used by people who meditate is to focus on the physical sensations you have while you are doing a particular task: the feel of the computer keys beneath your fingers as you type out a letter, the temperature of the room, the hardness of the chair you are sitting in, the sun streaming through the window. All these physical sensations help you to stay focused in the here and now and ensure that you put everything you have into what you are doing.

When you succeed, congratulate yourself. Enjoy the feelings of mastery that come with succeeding at something you have set out to do. The courage and sense of achievement you feel will help you take the next step, to a bigger goal, and so, step by step, you achieve your dreams.

Starting small and going slowly very definitely doesn't mean losing sight of your larger goals, however. For every person who comes a cropper because they have set their sights too high there are another ten who never fulfil themselves because they haven't aimed high enough. Setting limitations on your dreams too early on is stultifying. If you are constantly telling yourself that your dream is not achievable, you are not going to apply yourself wholeheartedly to reaching your goals. Far better to aim for the sky and settle for the far horizon, than to aim for the ground and end up never achieving your full potential. Remember: the secret of getting what you want is to think big and start small.

STEPS 5: CHECKING YOUR PROGRESS

As you proceed with your plan you will need to review it from time to time to check how well you are getting on. Checking your progress involves considering the action(s) you have taken, pinpointing any areas where you have been especially successful in achieving what you set out to do and also looking at areas where you didn't succeed so well. Doing this will help you identify any more information you need and strategies that worked particularly well. It will also enable you to indulge in one of the most satisfying parts of your *How To Get What You Want* campaign – giving yourself a pat on the back!

Use the following checklist:

> Was the final result what I intended?
> My original goal was ....
> The final result was ....

Look back at your original goal and see whether you met it. If you didn't, you need to think about why and what you could do to reach your intended goal. It may be back to the drawing board to refine your original plan, get more information and set better goals. Alternatively, you may be quite happy with what you have achieved. It might not have been what you set out to do, but the result might be even better.

> The following aspects of my plan worked particularly well:
> 1 ....
> 2 ....
> 3 ....

Try to pinpoint what was successful and why and think about how you can incorporate any especially successful strategies or techniques into your future plans. For instance, if you performed well at a job interview check off the particular points of what was successful: being on time, wearing the right clothes, your body language, the way you presented your CV, the way you talked about what you would be able to contribute to the job you were applying for, the fact that your father was managing director, or whatever. Plan to capitalise on your strengths the next time round.

> The following aspects of my plan caused me difficulty:
> 1 ....
> 2 ....
> 3 ....

Think about the problems and difficulties you encountered and how you might you solve them another time. See the section on problem solving in Chapter Seven and make plans to develop and improve the weak points of your plan. Remember, no plan is completely straightforward. Congratulate yourself on the parts of it that went well, forgive yourself for the parts of it that went badly, learn from them – and then move on.

> When putting your dreams into reality bear in mind the following points:
>
> - Have patience
> - Think big, start small
> - Be persistent
> - Cultivate a positive mental attitude
> - Don't compare yourself to other people
> - Enjoy!

TURNING YOUR DREAMS INTO REALITY ROUND UP

Now you know how to put your plans into action, you are ready to find out a bit more about two important assets that will help you to get what you want: time and money. The next two chapters will look at how you can create the time and the money to help you to turn your dreams into reality. But before you read on think about what you have learnt in this chapter and answer the following questions:

- ☐ Do you know where to find the information you need to put your dreams into action?
- ☐ Do you know how to set achievable goals?

> ☐ Will you know when you have reached them?
> ☐ Can you picture yourself turning your dreams into reality?

Yes? Then it's time to look at some more ways you can help yourself to get what you want.

CHAPTER FOUR
TIME FOR A CHANGE

Now you've had a a chance to look at some of the basic strategies in your *How To Get What You Want* campaign it's time to examine some of your assets and work out how to use them to help you achieve what you want. One asset that is vital in putting every plan into action is time. In this chapter you will discover where your time is going, how to beat the time wasters, and above all how to create the time you need to carry out your plans. As always, this involves taking a close look at where you are now.

Nothing can be worse than letting time slide away on meaningless or non-important things only to find one day that your whole life has slipped away without you doing anything you really wanted to do. It's a point you will have noticed we come back to repeatedly, but as with managing every aspect of your life, in order to use your time effectively you need to have a healthy dose of self-esteem. Having confidence in who you are is vital if you are to believe that time spent on doing the things you want to do is important.

Valuing yourself means you are able to set clear goals and targets, based on a knowledge of what makes you tick. If you've read this far you will already have a lot of ideas about this. So now let's have a look at how you can create the time you need to get what you want. But first, let's glance at how you spend your time.

WHERE DOES ALL THE TIME GO?

Your personal timetable is split in many different ways: time spent at work, at play, with your family, learning something new, 'me' time, time for your relationship, time spent with friends, and last, but not least, time 'just to stand and stare'. To see how you use time try the following:

> 1. On a page in your notebook write the days of the week down the left-hand side and write the hours of the day along the top.
>
> 2. At the end of each day, or at convenient intervals throughout it, note down what you did. Be specific and break it down as much as possible, e.g., 10 minutes going to shop to buy newspaper, 20 minutes making cup of tea and reading newspaper, 5 minutes washing and drying up mug and plate.
>
> 3. At the end of a week get three coloured crayons – say red, yellow and blue – and fill in your chart as follows:
>
> - Red: time spent on things that gave you the most satisfaction.
>
> - Yellow: time spent on things that gave you some satisfaction.
>
> - Blue: time spent on things that gave you no satisfaction.

Now look at your chart and see what it tells you about about the way you use time. If you have a lot of blue on your chart, it's high time to start making some changes. Look over the whole week and analyse how you spend your time. Draw a table – a circle with legs – and divide it up into slices of time. For example, a tenth spent on my family, a fifth spent on travelling, a quarter spent on working and so on. This is literally your timetable. The less time you are spending on the things you really want to do, the more frustration you are likely to feel. Now you know where all the time goes, you can start to create the time you need to do what you want to do.

Think about the following:

> - How well are you using your time?
> - Are you making the best use of your time and energy?
> - How much of your week do you spend doing activities you choose?
> - How much do you spend reacting to other people and events?
> - How much time did you really enjoy?

TAKING A NEW LOOK AT TIME

Time management, as the experts call it, is simply the art of arranging your time so that you spend it doing what you want rather than being at the mercy of other people and events over which you have no control. Wasting time, marking time, killing time, rather than using it to get on with what we want to do is one of the most important ways in which many of us hamper ourselves from reaching our goals.

If you spend all your time on wasteful activities so you never have the time to devote to things you find enhancing, or if you try to cram far too much into your life so that you are always rushing around, you create unnecessary stress. With time as with all your resources *you* need to choose how to use it.

The most difficult part of re-organising is keeping an open mind, because all of us have a tendency to think that the way we do things is the only possible way. It isn't: you always have a choice about how you use your time. You may choose not to live with the results of taking a particular choice. For example, if you always visit your mother every Sunday afternoon, you may decide you can't live with the guilt of disappointing her. If so, try to think of some alternatives: spending a couple of hours rather than the whole afternoon with her, arranging for your sister or another relative or friend to visit every other Sunday, or whatever. It's *your* choice.

There are a myriad ways of organising your time more effectively, so be flexible and be prepared to give some of them a try. Remember: to waste your time is ultimately to waste your life.

> Write in your notebook a list of promises to yourself about how you are going to use your time from now on:
>
> From now on, I am going to spend at least .... hours a week doing ....

USING YOUR BODY CLOCK

Everything you do uses up a certain amount of physical and/or mental energy. One of the simplest ways of creating more time for yourself is to harness your natural energy levels. For example, I find I am clearer and sharper first thing in the morning, more creative in the evening and pretty useless for anything very much between two and four in the afternoon. This means I can structure my timetable so that I work on things that need a sharp brain early in the morning, do routine and boring tasks between 2 and 4 p.m. and concentrate on tasks that need me to be creative or generate new ideas in the evening.

Energy levels don't just fluctuate over the course of a day. Many people who suffer from Seasonal Affective Disorder, (SAD) or seasonal depression, find that their energy levels are low during the long, dark days of winter. Women may find that their energy levels vary at different times of the month in association with their menstrual cycle. Being aware of your personal biorhythms can enable you to pinpoint your peak time for devoting yourself to the various tasks involved in getting what you want.

Find out your energy levels by going back to your weekly chart and filling in your personal 'up' and 'down' times. From now on, try to readjust your timetable so that you do the most important jobs at your peak time and leave the unimportant ones for the periods of the day when you are lacking in energy.

FINDING THE RIGHT TIME

Your energy level is also affected by your attitude towards the task in hand. You may find you use your time better if you are doing something interesting and satisfying, either in terms of material reward or mental satisfaction. On the other hand, boring, unstimulating jobs are often linked to doing things slowly and making inefficient use of time. However, it's not quite that straightforward. It's fatally easy to become so absorbed in doing something interesting that you waste time. If you have ever tried to sort out a cupboard or drawer containing old personal papers, only to find yourself reminiscing nostalgically as you browse through letters from friends, ancient holiday postcards and snaps some hours later, you'll know what I mean. On the other hand, faced with a boring, uninspiring job such as doing the ironing, you may be so eager to get it out of the way and get back to doing something you find interesting that you race through it.

A lot depends on your overall attitudes and beliefs: victims of the good old Puritan work ethic may be in the latter category, while the hedonists among us may be in the former. It all comes down to knowing yourself, finding the way you work best and then making sure that you allow for that in your plans.

Incidentally, there's absolutely nothing wrong with spending a whole day looking at photos and old letters – it might even provide you with some ideas about what you most enjoy doing – but make sure you plan it in to your schedule so you can enjoy it without feeling guilty.

TIME AND YOUR GOALS

Setting goals is much easier if you have a clear idea of when you want to achieve them by. If you structure your goals with time in mind, you will make better use of your time and achieve your goals more effectively.

To give an example, suppose you have let your financial affairs drift over the last few months. You'll never create the money to start your own business if you don't know where you are with your money now, so you need to get it sorted out. First of all you need to set yourself a goal.

Remember, goals should be as specific as possible. 'Sort out money this week' is not satisfactory: it doesn't tell you exactly what you need to do to set your affairs in order. Nor does it give you any idea *when* you will have finished. One way to monitor the progress of your goals is to write yourself a time checklist such as the following:

By the end of this week I will:

- Pay gas bill.
- Pay 'phone bill.
- Write to accountant.
- Check current account.
- Arrange transfer of funds from deposit account.

The checklist is vital because it tells you exactly what you have to do. It helps you know when to start and when you will have finished. You know you have to find the gas bill and the phone bill, phone or go to the bank, look through your bank statements and check them off against any cheques you have written. What's more, you know you have to have done these things by the end of the week. The checklist also helps you know when you have finished. At the end of the week you can check that you have done everything on the list.

THE JOB THAT NEVER GETS STARTED NEVER GETS FINISHED

One of the biggest secrets about getting what you want is to make time for it – and that applies just as much to creative endeavours as it does to the world of business. The novelist Anthony Burgess used to work seven days a week and wrote 3000 words a day – which almost certainly accounted for his prolific output. In the case of a novel, the final outcome of the plot may be mysterious even to the author. But whatever happens the novel has to be written – and that means making time.

CREATING MORE TIME

The main way to create more time is what the experts called prioritising – what you and I call putting first things first. All this means is simply setting down your goals in order of their importance. Things that happen in life fall into two main kinds: ones that you know are going to happen and ones that crop up.

The things that you know are going to happen are the ones over which you have the most control, and which can often help you to achieve what you want in key areas of your life. The things that crop up have to be dealt with as quickly as possible to get them out of the way as you can, so plan in some free time slots for them.

To look at how you might do this:

> 1. List the jobs and activities you have to do that have a deadline or have to be done by a certain date. These are your urgent jobs.
>
> 2. Next list the jobs and activities you have to do that could have serious consequences if left undone such as going to have a cervical smear or visiting the dentist. These are your important jobs.
>
> 3. Finally, list the jobs and activities that if not done urgently could have serious consequences. For instance if you don't pay your 'phone bill within the next seven days you risk your telephone being cut off. These are your important and urgent jobs.

From now on, aim to avoid letting things fall into list three by planning ahead. For example if you have a tendency to forget to pay your 'phone bill, don't wait until you get the red bill informing you that you are about to be cut off. Make a note in your diary of when you have to pay it by, or arrange for your bill to be paid automatically.

Now look at the jobs in list one. Some items on this list may be able to be shelved altogether. Which ones can wait? Which ones will go away if you don't do them? Which ones do you have to get done? Write these into your diary, making sure you leave enough time to complete them. This leaves jobs or activities in list two: the important things. This is where you put the things you want. These are things you know are going to happen, and by and large choose to make happen, which are also important to you.

LEAVE YOURSELF ENOUGH TIME

Many of us – particularly journalists and writers! – can't work without deadlines. However, it is vital to allow yourself enough time to do what you plan to do. Otherwise you risk having to rush or botch a job, which is likely be counterproductive in the long run. Things usually take twice as long as you imagine – allowing for things going wrong, trains breaking down, unexpected problems and so on – so when setting yourself a time goal, try to be realistic. Write down an estimate of how long you think it will take – and then double it.

LEARN TO NEGOTIATE

However efficient you are, you are not Superman and you can't hope to do everything. If it's apparent that you can't meet a deadline without delaying something more important, then it is often possible to negotiate some leeway. For example, you may decide to write a letter or make a phone call apologising or requesting more time to pay that unpaid bill. Many of us put off such tasks out of fear of the consequences. In fact most people you deal with would prefer to know if something is going to be late or if you are going to be unable to do something.

STICKING TO YOUR PLAN

Those of us who have difficulty sticking to plans often have to apply a combination of stick and carrot to help ourselves follow through. One of the best ways to increase motivation is to involve other people in your plans. By telling someone else what you intend to do, you give others the chance to support and help you if they can. At the same time, it's more difficult to get out of something you have made public. For example, if you are determined to lose two stones in weight, joining a slimming club, starting a diet with a friend or joining a gym where your progress is assessed at various intervals by an instructor are all good ways of helping strengthen your resolve. Rewarding yourself at regular intervals when you have achieved your goals is another powerful motivator. So, if you are slimming, promising yourself a new outfit when you have lost 14 lbs can help you stick to the straight and narrow when you feel tempted to give in and eat a big cream cake.

EASY WAYS TO MAKE MORE TIME

As well as learning to prioritise, there are several other simple yet effective ways of creating more time for yourself. These are some of them:

- Get up an hour earlier.
- Go to bed an hour later.
- Put something less important off.
- Learn to do routine tasks faster.
- Use time spent travelling or waiting for trains, or at the doctor's surgery, for reading, dreaming or writing. Don't spend it raging over the delay!

Remember all you need is a little time each day.

KEEPING A BALANCE

The happiest and most fulfilled people are those who achieve a balance between all the different strands in their life. Inevitably, there will be occasions when you choose to spend more time or energy on one particular area. For instance, if you are on holiday with your partner you can forget about time spent with friends, except perhaps for sending them a postcard, and concentrate on enjoying yourself and the time you spend together.

Other times when time may get out of balance are at specific turning points in your life: moving house, going to college or returning to learning, having a baby, a new relationship or change in an existing relationship. You can learn more about dealing with turning points or life transitions in the companion to this book, *The Survivor Personality*.

The best way to cope with imbalances in your timetable is to prepare both yourself and others who are likely to be affected that they are about to happen and will demand more of your time and energy than usual. This way it's possible to keep both yourself and others happy. For example, if your partner is expecting a baby and you are likely to need some time off work, arrange it well in advance and plan your work schedule in the meantime. People are usually amazingly tolerant as long as they know what to expect. A prolonged imbalance in the way you spend your time is likely to take its toll on your relationships, career prospects as well as your overall health and well-being. In this case you need to find ways of dealing with the extra stress and tension such an imbalance invariably causes.

Check your balance: when you make your list of things to do, check that your daily list includes goals from each area of your timetable. By setting yourself goals that reflect each area of your life you will feel more fulfilled.

BEAT THE TIME WASTERS

Time wasters are the things that sap your energy, leaving you no time to do the things you want to do. Once you know what they are – look back at your timetable and see where your time goes – it's simply a question of thinking up creative solutions.

BEAT the tyranny of the 'phone. Take the 'phone off the hook or unplug it. Put on the answerphone and monitor your calls. If even this is too disrupting, plug the answerphone into a socket in another room and turn down the sound. Leave a message on the answerphone saying when you will be available. Only return the calls you have to return; otherwise, let other people call you. Make an appointment with yourself to catch up on your 'phone calls and schedule it in. Arrange to 'phone relatives and friends who you keep in touch with regularly at a specific time each week or day so you don't get interrupted when you are trying to do something else. Let other people know when it is convenient to 'phone you. Do a whole load of your 'phone calls together, say on Sunday evening or some other convenient time.

BEAT disorganisation. If you haven't done so already invest in a Filofax or diary. Write down everything you have to do the next day in your diary before you go to bed at night. Tick things off as you do them during the day. Make lists: a list of things you have to do at work, a list of things you have to do at home, a list of people you have to telephone. Don't put things down – put them away! Put things away where you can find them the minute you have finished with them. Devise a filing system. The best systems are simple to operate. Choose how you are going to categorise things: alphabetically A–Z, by subject or theme, by, colour or some other method.

BEAT the nice girl/boy mentality. Too many of us do things we don't want to do because we want to be liked. The syndrome often afflicts women especially, probably because they are brought up to please people, but can affect men too. Learn to say 'No' to things you don't want to do or that aren't really important. You have to be prepared to risk other people feeling annoyed or hurt if you disrupt their plans, but your real friends will understand, and the others? Who needs them? Having a healthy self-esteem will help you withstand disapproval.

BEAT overcommitment. Become aware of how much you can do in the time available. Prioritise, prioritise, prioritise! When someone asks you to do something ask yourself:

- 'Is what I am doing really necessary?'
- 'Is this the best way to use my time?'
- 'Is this what I really want to do?'

If the answers are 'No', don't do them, or schedule them in for non-peak times.

BEAT your 'shoulds' and 'oughts'. Don't feel you must do something just because you have always done it or always do it in a certain way. Look at the things you do routinely and brainstorm some alternative ways of dealing with them. How often do you need to perform these tasks? Is there another way you could do them? Could you do them faster? Could you delegate them? Clarify your standards and your expectations – and challenge them. Some examples: must you always dust the skirting board when you clean the sitting room? Who would notice if you didn't do it? Is it important? Could you dust just once a month for the same effect? Must you always take your daughter to Brownies every Tuesday evening when you want to do a particular evening class? Could you arrange a swap with another parent?

Time waste check:

> 1. Write down five things which you feel rob you of the time you want to spend on other things.
>
> 2. Now write down all the possible solutions. Don't censor your solutions, however fanciful they may seem. Once you start to think about them they may suggest more realistic solutions, but how can you know unless you have thought about them?
>
> 3. Now select one of those solutions and think it through. If you do it what will this mean – for you, for other people?
>
> 4. The next step is to try it out. Decide how long you will need to try out this solution, then check back after this set period to see whether it is working, whether it needs to be adapted or scrapped altogether, whether you need to try something else. If you do this regularly you'll soon find you are making better use of your time.

THE TIME OF YOUR LIFE

Now you have read this chapter and are in a position to start making better use of your time, there's one further bit of time planning which is vital to getting what you want. This is your life plan and it's designed to make sure that you start spending your time in the way you want to spend it – for the rest of your life.

Put aside a time every year when you will look at your life and where you are going. I like to do mine when I go away on holiday and feel calm and relaxed enough to spend some time visualising what I want my future to be. I also like to do it with a friend so we can bounce ideas off each other. It's a really enjoyable exercise to do, so pick a time when you are feeling relaxed, pour yourself a drink you enjoy, get your notebook and a pen, and get started.

Answer the following questions:

- What do I want to be doing ten years from now?
- What do I want to be doing five years from now?

Think about the following areas: your health, appearance, social life, leisure, travel plans, family, friends, colleagues, work, voluntary work and anything else that is important to you. These are your long-term goals and they are important, because what you choose to do now will affect what you do in the future.

Now for both questions consider:

- How is what I want to do different from what I am doing now?
- What can I start doing now to get where I want to be in . . . years' time? (Write down some goals, bearing in mind the rules we looked at earlier.)
- What barriers might prevent me from achieving what I want to do? (Write down ones you think you can do something about and those you think are out of your control – we'll be looking at these in a later chapter.)

Now look back over the last year (once you've done this exercise once you can look back in your notebook) and check how well you achieved the goals you set yourself last year. Tick the ones you have achieved and think about whether to scrap the others or transfer them to this year's list.

TIME FOR A CHANGE ROUND UP

Now you know how to manage your time better you are ready to examine another important asset: money. But first, check what you have learnt about time. Look at the list below and answer the following questions.

> ☐ Do you know where your time goes?
> ☐ Are you aware of your time wasters?
> ☐ Do you know how to make time to do the things that are important to you?
> ☐ Can you picture yourself doing what you want to do in five years' time and in ten years' time?

Yes? Then let's look at how you can get the money you want.

CHAPTER FIVE
CONJURING THE CASH

Like it or not, we live in a world that runs on money and whatever you choose to do you will need to think about how to finance it. Money is an asset just like time. Many of us (myself included) bury our heads in the sand where money is concerned. The only time we worry about it is when it runs out. The good news is that once you become aware of your spending habits and where your money goes, then, just as with time, you can take charge of your finances and start making your money work for you. Once you have done that you will find that you can actually create money – just as you can create time and any other of the resources you need to get what you want. And that's a very exciting thought.

CULTIVATING A POSITIVE ATTITUDE TOWARDS MONEY

As with everything else self-confidence is vital if you are to make your money work for you. If you are worried about losing your job, that your business will fail or that you will never find another job, you are unlikely to be imaginative about the ways in which you can use your money. Cultivating a positive belief in yourself and your ability to find the money to finance your dream will enable you to relax and think about new ways both of acquiring money and spending it on what you desire. It's amazing how once you have decided to be the one holding the reins, the money side of life starts to take care of itself. Managing money is easy, once you take matters into your own hands and start to take control. Something else

CONJURING THE CASH · 57

to bear in mind is this: it's not so much how much money you have, but what you do with it, that counts.

THAT'S THE WAY THE MONEY GOES

The first step in starting to manage your money is to examine your present financial position – where you are today and where you want to be tomorrow. You will also look at the personal and financial factors that have led you to your present position. How you manage your money reflects not just the everyday practicalities like having to pay the gas bill and going to the supermarket, it is also a mirror of your overall approach to life. Your personality is crucial in the way you approach money and this affects getting what you want. Have a look at the following characters and see if any of them ring a bell:

- **Happy Harriet**. You live for the moment. The moment you get any cash in your hot little hands you rush out and spend it. You believe money is there to be enjoyed, and enjoy it you do: your wardrobe is full of clothes, often bought on the spur of the moment. Your house is stuffed with beautiful objects picked up as you cruise the shops. You spend money on holidays, eating out, presents, you name it . . . You may be hampered from getting what you want because you never have the money – you've already frittered it away. Your attitude: the future? I'll think about it when it comes.
- **Cautious Christine**. You are a cautious planner, who uses money as a comfort blanket. There's a personal health plan in case you get ill, savings for emergencies, a pension for your old age, a mortgage that is well on the way to being paid up. You budget carefully and only buy things when you know you can afford them. You have the money but you may be hampered from getting what you want by being too cautious to commit your money to any, as you see it, 'risky' project. Your attitude: look after the pennies and the pounds will take care of themselves.
- **Debt-bound Debbie**. You struggle to get by on an income that barely supports your basic needs. Red letters and final demands

drop through your letter box with every post. You worry constantly about money and how you will manage. Yet, somehow, although you try, you get deeper and deeper into a spiral of debt. You are hampered from getting what you want because all your spare cash goes on paying off your debts. Your attitude: what am I going to do?

Do you recognise yourself? The secret of creating the money you need to finance what you want is to work with your personality rather than against it and to take control of the way you manage your finances. Experts divide money into two main categories: capital and income. Capital is the money you keep under your mattress, in a savings account, as investments either of the cash variety or as things – your house, your grandmother's jewellery, the painting you bought for a song which turned out to be a famous Picasso, in other words everything you own. Capital can also take the form of anticipated assets – the endowment policy you took out, the pension you have been saving for ever since you started work, your parents' house, the nest egg you hope will come your way if your Great-Uncle Herbert ever pops it.

Income is the money that literally 'comes in' to your life. It can be earned, usually by working, or unearned, money you get as interest from your savings, benefits or maintenance. Your income is closely tied to your commitments – the money you have to pay out to pay the taxman, the gas bill, the mortgage and so on. Your commitments may also include the interest on your overdraft, the bank loan you took out to buy a new computer, the hire purchase on your car and any credit or store cards you own. Other commitments include things you may choose to spend your money on – travelling, your clothes, children's school fees, servicing your car. (Yes, you do *choose* to spend your money on these things!) The link between these two forms of money – capital and income – is your lifestyle, the way you live your life. So, you may, like Cautious Christine, choose to use some of your income to save up for the things you want to do. On the other hand, you may be like Happy Harriet and spend your money on the good things in life. Ideally, if you want to get what you want, you should be aiming for a combination of the two. And this comes back to thinking about what you want out of life and the sort of person you would like to be. To do this, and to start managing your money so that you can do what you want, you need to take a cool look at who you are.

YOUR MONEY AND YOUR LIFE

Money tends to play a different role at different stages in our lives. At each stage your needs will dictate both your income and capital and also your attitude towards your money and what you choose to spend it on. The following represents a typical pattern:

- **Carefree childhood**. This is the time of life when most people worry least about money and when your attitudes towards money are formed. Many of these attitudes will come from your parents. Any cash comes mainly as pocket money from your parents or as Christmas or birthday presents from grandparents and others. You may have been the sort of child who rushed out to squander all her pocket money on sweets the moment she got it and then had to ask for a sub for next week (a future Happy Harriet), or the sort who carefully put every penny in her piggy bank (a future Cautious Christine). As you get older, you may earn some money from doing odd jobs. If you are lucky, your parents and other relatives may have invested some money to build up capital for when you grow up.
- **Young, single and . . . broke**. In your 20s you are (probably) in your first paid work, and your main aim may be to earn as much money as possible and then spend it. Savings schemes and pension plans seem irrelevant and the only type of saving that may hold any sort of attraction is that of saving up for a deposit for a home. Now is the time to start establishing a good relationship with your bank or building society. It could pay dividends later if you need a loan to help you do something you want.
- **Truly, madly, deeply**. As you reach your 30s you may get married or settle down with a permanent partner. If you do, you will have the luxury of two incomes which means money for

spending on the good things of life – holidays, restaurant meals, entertaining. Your main investment is likely to be part of your nest-building: buying your own apartment or house and furnishing it. Property values are not as certain as they were, but buying property still represents one of the biggest investments you are likely to make in your life.

- **Babylove**. If you go on to have children your income – and your attitude towards your income – is likely to be stretched. Spending on meals out and exotic holidays gives way to paraphernalia such as baby buggies, toys, estate cars (as the family grows) and, if you both still work outside the home, childcare. There may also be school fees to take into account. With all these expenses there may be little left to think about saving or spending on what you want. Nonetheless, there are still ways you can create money. If you have chosen not to have children this can be a time when you are at the peak of your earning. Now is the time to think about spending some of your income on investments, a pension plan, and creating money to allow you to do some of the things you want, both now and in the future.

- **Empty nest**. Between your mid-40s and mid-50s, the children leave home and the pressure on your finances usually starts to ease a little. You may have paid off most of your mortage and got most of the possessions you want. Now is the time to enjoy a higher standard of living. It's also a good time to think about some of the life changes you want to make. For people without children this is another good period and you may be able to ease off somewhat in your job and maybe even think about doing something that is less well paid – but more satisfying. It's also a time when you begin to believe that one day you might be old, so now is the time too to review your provision for the future.

- **Retirement**. Conventional retirement brings another dramatic change in your attitude to money. Suddenly your income is dramatically cut. If you are healthy, now is another time when you might be thinking about ways in which you could change your life, by starting your own small business for example, and give yourself a cash injection. You may also want to take into account how you might help provide for the financial future of people who are important to you, such as your children and grandchildren, by making a will.

Your position on the financial life cycle will influence both your attitudes towards money and your needs. For instance, do you want to spend as much as possible now, or would you like to invest some of your money so it will grow? Your answers will be very different if you are at the beginning of your working life or if you are facing retirement. Time also plays a part. Do you have the time – and inclination – to be actively involved in managing your money, or would you prefer a financial plan that runs itself?

More and more women these days have chosen to delay or not to have children. In this case, the typical life cycle is somewhat different. Not having children can be a positive choice, which allows you the time and money to concentrate on getting more of the things you want to do. For example, you may find yourself in middle age, having had time to concentrate on building a high-powered and well-paid career with money to spare. How will you spend it? On buying a cottage in the country or abroad? On setting up your own business? On investing it so you can retire early? The possibilities are endless.

WORK AND MONEY

Your job and employment status are closely linked to your money – and the way you think about it. Consider the following:

- Are you in a full-time or part-time job?
- Are you unemployed?
- Are you self-employed?
- Are you retired?

Your concerns about money will vary depending on your answers to these questions. For instance, if you work for an employer: is your career on the way up, static, or on the way down? What is your earning potential? What is the likelihood of promotion? If you are self-employed: what is the market for your work? Is it static, increasing or decreasing? Can you open up new markets? Will they be better paid/worse paid? What sort of provision have you made for illness and retirement? If you are unemployed: is it a temporary situation? Have you chosen not to have a job? How long have you been without paid work? Do you want paid work?

Some of the analyses you have already done will help you answer these questions. You will find others in Chapter Eight.

YOUR MONEY AND YOUR RELATIONSHIPS

Your relationships – whether you have a partner, are married or planning to get married, are divorced, separated or single – play a large part in your financial thinking. All relationships involve costs – financial as much as emotional – and it's important to bear these in mind when thinking about the way you manage your money. You need to consider not just where you are in your relationships now, but also where you want to be in the future. Would you and your partner like to take a year off for that round-the-world trip? What will happen if you decide to live together? Should you draw up a cohabitation contract? Are you planning to get married? If so, think about drawing up a pre-marital contract that sets out your financial rights. Such measures may seem callous when you are in the first flush of love, but can save you a lot of pain and agony should your relationship be one of the one in three that doesn't survive. Do you want to settle down and perhaps have children? If you have them, what financial demands will they place on you? Are your parents or your partner's parents independent, or might you have to consider building a granny flat? What might happen if your daughter's shaky relationship finally hits the rocks? Thinking about such questions can help you plan for the future so you are not taken by surprise.

WHERE ARE YOU NOW?

Remember the next stage in turning your dreams into reality (after dreaming) is to gather information. Well, now you are ready to take a cool look at your financial situation.

INCOME AND OUTGOINGS

First, look at your total income and outgoings. You will need a pen and your notebook.

> 1. At the top of a page write down your age, number of children and any other dependants and whether you are single, separated, married, divorced, widowed. On each of two pages create three columns headed: 'Description', 'Where I am now', and 'Anticipated change'.
>
> 2. On the first page write 'My income' and write down everything you have coming in. Include your salary or wages, income from your business, maintenance, benefits, pension, interest on any investments, and any other sources of income like windfalls. Now add up the total and write it down at the end of the page.
>
> 3. On the next page (this may actually run over several pages) write 'My outgoings' and write down everything you have to pay out. Include all your regular living expenses such as rent and mortgage payments, council tax, water rates, TV rental/licence fees, your telephone bills, gas bills, electricity bills, building and contents insurance on your house and any other insurance premiums; your household expenses such as food, drinks, and basics for the home, meals out, cleaning and gardening, pets, childcare; travel expenses such as your car or public transport, taxis, insurance, MOT/repairs and so on; your social/self expenses such as entertainment, clothes, cosmetics, holidays, magazines and newspapers, books, records, luxuries, Christmas, birthday presents, addictions, such as collecting antique sports cars or going Latin American dancing every night – and anything else you can think of. Now add all these up together. This is the money you spend.

> 4. Now subtract your total outgoings from your total income and write in the figure.

WHAT YOU OWN AND WHAT YOU OWE

Now let's have a look at your assets – what you own – and your liabilities – what you owe.

> 1. Take two more pages in your notebook and head each one: 'Current value' and 'Any expected change'.
>
> 2. On the first page, write 'What I own' and list all your capital. Include your home (if you own it) or other property, furniture and equipment with their approximate value, clothes, antiques, jewellery, investments, savings accounts, endowment policies, pension policies and anything else which can be converted into hard cash. Now add all these up. These are your assets.
>
> 3. On the next page write 'What I owe' and list the outstanding amount on your mortgage, loans, overdraft, credit or store cards and other credit accounts, tax and any other outstanding debts. Now add them all up. These are your liabilities.

ANALYSING YOUR MONEY

Try not to be frightened at this stage – remember you're in the driving seat and getting information is the first step towards making changes. Now you have some hard information on which to base your financial plans, the next step is to analyse that information, to turn it into working knowledge on which you can base a financial plan of action. You may be quite happy with the way things are looking, in which case you don't have to go any further. On the other hand, you may feel you want to make more money to finance your *How To Get What You Want* campaign. First of all, think about your income and ways you might increase it – I'll be making a few suggestions later on. Now think about your outgoings and ways in which you could adjust them – don't do anything at this stage, simply think, or possibly brainstorm, some possible solutions. If you have debts to pay off, think about these. You'll find some more suggestions later in this chapter.

Think, too, about what provisions you have made for the future – for illness or incapacity, retirement and (hard though it may be to contemplate) death. If you haven't made any provision now is the time to do so. There are several good books on money management and most newspapers carry weekly advice on personal finance. Another thing you could do is to contact an independent financial adviser, who can recommend various money management plans and also help you if you are in the fortunate position of having money to invest.

Finally think about the things you *want* to do – travel the world, start a business, buy a villa in Greece or whatever.

FINANCING YOUR DREAM

You are now ready to make an action plan that will create the money you need to do what you want. To do this you don't need to be a financial wizard. There are two main ways:

- Increasing your income.
- Rebalancing your expenditure.

Before you say 'I can't' to either of these stop – and think. As with time, so with money. Basically you choose. So now is the time to think about how you might generate some extra income. Brainstorm the possibilities and then examine them one by one. Some suggestions:

> - Change your job if you work for an employer. If there's no possibility of earning more money in your present job you may have to think about changing it (see Chapter Eight)

- Examine the possibilities for promotion. If there is a chance of moving up in your career, find out what you have to do to get on the ladder – take a course, take on extra work, talk to the boss. Make an action plan

- If you are self-employed think about taking on better paid projects, opening up new markets, making better use of your time. Be ruthless and cut out poorly paid jobs to create more time for better paid ones

- Take on an extra or part-time job in your spare time. Make something, sell something, work in a shop, a bar, a restaurant . . .

- Cash in an insurance policy or endowment

- Sell something – the car, your grandmother's jewellery, your house – in other words release some of your assets. Think about moving to a cheaper area, or buying a smaller house. Do you really need a car? Could you manage with an older one, or with public transport?

- Borrow. Think about all the possibilities – could you borrow from a friend (think about the implications of this and how you might pay him/her back), the bank, a building society? Do you have an overdraft? Investigate bank and other forms of loans (seek the help of a financial adviser if necessary)

SAVING MONEY SO YOU CAN SPEND

The next step is to examine your expenditure with a fine-tooth comb as there are usually ways you can cut back if you put your mind to it. You don't have to have a holiday in the Caribbean, you could go to Cornwall, exchange your home or go self-catering. You don't have to spend money on expensive designer clothes, you could make your own, buy in designer second-hand shops, haunt jumble sales and charity shops. You could cut down on newspapers by watching the news on TV, you could save money on books by getting them out of the library.

A tip: 'Superwoman' Shirley Conran has this to say about cutting down on your expenditure. 'Never cut down on what makes your life worth living: if you have chocolate cake for Sunday tea, don't switch to buns; if your one joy is playing squash, don't hang up your racquets. The trick is to economise in a big way on something boring . . .' You have been told!

- *Jim and Judy had always wanted to travel to India. Once their children were at university they decided this was the time to go. These are the steps they took to create the money:*
  - *Monitored the input and outflow of finances by a weekly review of their spending and income.*
  - *Cut down money spent on eating out by eating in restaurants only once a week and spending no more than £20 a week.*
  - *Judy took on extra work researching a book for a friend of hers.*
  - *They opened a special 'India Fund' high-interest deposit account – and put in £200 each month.*

MANAGING DEBT

Most of us have been brought up to regard being in debt as shameful, and this is one of the reasons it can be so difficult to deal with. Burying your head in the sand will not help; you must face up to it and tackle it. First of all, try to banish all those old messages about the wickedness of debt – after all, what does the Chancellor of the Exchequer do if he doesn't have enough money to go round? He borrows it – in other words he creates a debt. Some people can live with the thought of owing money, others can't. It's as simple as that. All you have to do is decide which you are and plan your money management accordingly. Debt is only a bad thing if you let it rule you. The secret of dealing with your debts is to manage them. Here are a few suggestions:

- Make a list of all the people you owe money to and how much you owe each of them. Then work out how much you can (realistically) pay and write to them all suggesting you pay in instalments. Most people, even that traditional ogre, the taxman, will accept this these days

- Always keep your creditors (the people you owe money to) informed. That way they have more confidence in you
- Be realistic about what you can afford to pay off – don't underestimate your cost of living – it's better to suggest paying less rather than breaking your promises
- Don't borrow money to pay off your debts – unless it's from someone reputable like your bank manager
- Consider consulting a Debt Advice Agency or self-help group such as Wallet Watchers for people who are in debt

KEEPING A BALANCE

There's no right or wrong way to manage your money, only the way that is right for you. Your knowledge of yourself can help you in financial planning just as it can in every other area of getting what you want. For example, there's little point in buying a farmhouse in France if you like to go to a different place for your holidays each year, nor is there any point in buying a flash new car if you are quite happy with your old banger or going by public transport.

Similarly, there's absolutely no reason to make yourself miserable by splashing out on meals out, expensive clothes and a lavish social life if you are worrying all the time about the future, nor in hoarding every spare bit of cash for some distant old age. It's all a question of getting the balance right – deciding what you want to get out of life and setting this against your natural caution or lack of it. After all, your money is only worth anything if it helps you to achieve what you want, whatever your ambitions. So take charge, remember you are in the driving seat and don't let your money dictate the direction in which you go. Establish what is right for you – and then go for it.

CONJURING THE CASH ROUND UP

Now you know how to manage both your time and your money you are well on the way to getting what you want. In the next chapter, you are going to find out how you can improve your communication skills so as to ask more effectively for what you want. But for now let's just check on what you have learnt in this chapter. Look at the list below and answer the following questions.

- [ ] Do you know where your money comes from?
- [ ] Do you know where your money goes?
- [ ] Do you feel happy that your attitude towards money matches your patterns of expenditure?
- [ ] Do you feel confident that you can create the money you want to finance what you want?

Right. Then let's examine how you can get on better with the people around you.

CHAPTER SIX
TALKING ABOUT WHAT YOU WANT

Letting other people know what you want, knowing how to put a point across in a way that ensures they understand, learning how to express your thoughts, feelings and emotions to other people, listening to what others have to say in return – in other words good communication – is vital if you are to get what you want.

Good communication – letting other people in on what you are thinking – is the secret of ensuring that other people notice you in your daily life at work, rest and play, and of making friends and other relationships. Poor communication – the inability to put your thoughts and feelings across to others – can leave you feeling lonely, miserable, misunderstood and frustrated.

But communicating effectively is about more than just the words you use when you open your mouth to speak. It is also about being sensitive to what your own and other people's body language – things like posture, facial expression, gestures – tells you about whether your message is getting across. It means being aware of your listener as a separate individual with different needs, interests, ambitions, aims and ways of seeing the world. The style of your communication – both what you say and how you say it – must be suited to the situation you are in and the relationship you have with the person you are communicating with. For example, you wouldn't dream of asking your bank manager for a loan in the same way that you might try to cajole your partner into spending an extra hour in bed on Saturday morning! Learning to communicate effectively can make all the difference between wanting something – and not getting it – and being able to shape your life as you desire it.

ARE YOU GETTING YOUR MESSAGE ACROSS?

Psychologists have analysed the skills used by people who communicate effectively – and are therefore good at getting what they want – compared with those used by people who don't communicate well – and who frequently fail to get what they want. How do you score? Tick the ones that apply to you:

> When trying to get something I want:
> 1. a) I usually know what I want to say.
>
>   b) I am often not clear about what I want to say or who I should ask/tell.
>
> 2. a) I know how to grab the attention of my audience/listener.
>
>   b) I often fail to enlist the attention of my audience/listener.
>
> 3. a) I am able to establish and maintain relationships with people when I want to.
>
>   b) I frequently fail to get to know the people I want to know and my relationships are characterised by misunderstanding.
>
> 4. a) When opening a conversation/communication I usually know what to say to whet the appetite of my audience/listener.
>
>   b) When opening a conversation or communication the person/people I am talking to frequently appear bored or inattentive.

5. a) I am able to choose the best way of getting my message across from a range of options. I know when to be angry, assertive, sensitive, sympathetic.

b) I feel I often don't put my message across very effectively: I laugh or cry when I am angry, I am too firm when I intend to be gentle or persuasive, I shout when someone doesn't respond to what I am saying.

6. a) I know how to listen and I am usually aware of what the body language of the other person is telling me.

b) I am usually so intent on getting my message across that I often fail to notice if someone turns away/switches off/is angry.

7. a) I tend to adjust my message to the way the person I am talking to is responding to me.

b) I know what I want to say and I say it in exactly the same way no matter how the person I am talking to responds.

8. a) I usually think about the best time and place to start a conversation/make a particular point.

b) I frequently seem to pick the wrong moment to start a conversation/make a point.

9. a) I feel able to ask for what I want or put my point across in a way that is clear and to the point.

b) I often get waylaid, waffle or stray off the point in conversation or communication.

10. a) I feel able to ask for more information if I haven't understood what is being said.

b) I frequently pretend to have understood something that someone tells me even though I haven't really done so.

> 11.a) I know how to sign off a conversation or communication.
>
> b) I often have difficulty in ending a conversation or communication.

How did you get on? If you ticked mainly 'a's', congratulations – you are already an excellent communicator and well on the way to getting what you want. If you ticked mainly 'b's' you could do with brushing-up on communication skills.

Now let's look at a few of these skills in more detail and try to discover ways in which you can develop them.

THINKING ABOUT WHAT YOU WANT TO SAY

Having a clear idea of what you want to say before you say it will help you to come to the point quickly and enable your message to be received clearly. Explanation can follow at a later stage if necessary. But in the first instance try to get your point across as clearly and briefly as possible. So, if you are asking boss for a pay rise, once you've made a time to see him or her come straight to the point and say, 'I've come to ask you for a rise.' You can then go on to explain what a wonderful person you are and why you deserve more money.

If you aren't clear in your own mind about what you really want to say or ask for, you may wrap up your message in unnecessary waffle. As a result the person you are talking to may switch off or become impatient, or you may come away wondering why you were misunderstood.

The same goes for non-verbal communication (body language). For example, if you are telling your nearest and dearest you are having an affair with his/her best friend and that it's all over between you it's probably best not to do it after a cosy tête-à-tête followed by a night of passionate love making.

Some points to consider:

- Who are you talking to? Adjust your message and the way you want to say it accordingly. For example (although there might be some similarities in approach) you would approach a bolshy toddler to ask him to pick up his toys from the floor rather differently from the way you would approach a rebellious teenager who you had discovered was dropping 'E'.

- What result are you hoping for? Think about what you are hoping to achieve and adjust your message accordingly. For example, if you order a 'terrible two-year-old' to pick up his toys *now*, you're more likely to receive a defiant, 'No,' than if you get down to his level and start helping him to pick up his toys and put them in the toy box.
- What approach is likely to be most effective? In other words, what communication style would work best? Should you adopt a softly, softly approach or would a more direct, assertive method of getting your point across be more successful? For instance, if you are asking your bank manager for a loan to start up a new business you are more likely to meet with success if you go prepared with a business plan, cash flow forecasts and other evidence that you have thought the whole thing through than if you breeze in with absolutely no idea of how much you want to borrow and how you might pay it back.
- Where is the best place to say what you want? For instance, if you want to tell your boss that you are thinking of going freelance, should you raise the subject while you're having a friendly lunch in the staff restaurant, or would it be better to ask for a quiet word in his office where you can have the time and space to explain your plans and enlist any help he is able to offer in the way of contacts, freelance work and so on?
- Do you have your main points clear in your own mind? Check that what you want to say is clear, that there is no ambiguity and that you have the correct facts or information to back up your argument. Make sure that if the other person is required to act in some way as a result of what you have said, this is understood. For example, when winding up a meeting, 'So James is going to prepare a report on such and such within the next ten days; Maggie, you are going to speak to the accounts department; and Louise, you're going to fix a date and time for our next meeting and let us all know.'

YOU – AND YOUR MESSAGE

Believing in yourself is vital in getting what you want, and not surprisingly self-image plays a large part in getting you – and what you want – across effectively. If you have a poor opinion of yourself you may only ever get what you want by accident – because your lack of confidence will be loud and clear in the way you speak and project yourself. If you don't believe in yourself, how can you expect other people to?

Remember, every time you open your mouth to speak to another person you are expressing yourself, whether you are aware of it or not. The clothes you wear, the way you stand or hold yourself, the tone and pitch of your voice, speak volumes about the person you are and the way you feel about yourself.

If you have a poor self-image, you may be prickly and insecure in your dealings with other people. You may feel that what you have to say isn't sufficiently important to interest others and speak too quietly or in a rush. Concerned to uphold your shaky confidence in yourself, you may have difficulty in accepting criticism, admitting to mistakes or voicing your feelings, just in case you put your foot in it.

The good news is that if you don't feel good about yourself you can improve the way you feel. You've already started just by picking up this book and you'll learn a good deal more as you read on. For the time being think about the following:

- Are your clothes right for the situation? How casual or smart are you? And what impression do your clothes convey about you? That pretty floral dress may be fine for a summer picnic in the park, but is it really right for this business meeting? Those jeans may be fine if you are working in a creative field but not if you are trying to make a career in banking. Pay attention to what you wear and make sure you dress for the occasion. This can be especially important if you are doing business in a foreign country where you are not so familiar with the dress code. If in doubt, ask. However you choose to dress make sure you are clean and well-groomed.
- Watch your body language. Research has shown that body language doesn't lie. For example, if you ask someone the way

in the street and he says, 'Turn right,' but points left, nine times out of ten the non-verbal gesture is the one you should pay attention to. Body language – posture, gesture, facial expression – becomes even more important if what someone is saying seems to contradict their body language. For example, people who try to persuade you they are speaking the truth, but fiddle with their hands or move their feet uneasily under the table, are not likely to convince you. The experts call such signals 'non-verbal leakage' and being aware of them, both in yourself and others, can help you read messages and convey them much more accurately. One way in which fortune tellers and clairvoyants appear to know so much about us is that they are skilled at reading non-verbal signs. So when you are talking to someone, remember not to slouch, to look your listener in the eye (averting your eyes can look shifty even though it may simply be a sign of shyness or embarrassment), and to hold yourself in a straight but not rigid posture. Adopt an open posture – crossing your arms and legs can make you appear unapproachable and defensive. Face your listener, but don't position yourself directly across from someone as it could suggest you are in opposition.

- Try to create an environment that shows you at your best. Where will you be talking to the person? In your own sitting room? In this case, sitting next to each other at right angles is often a good way to position furniture to create a relaxed atmosphere. Or more formally across a desk – for example, if you are meeting your bank manager or doctor? Of course, if you are on your own territory it isn't difficult to arrange your environment to suit the circumstances of your meeting. However, even in more formal situations it may be possible to make small adjustments that create a more empowering atmosphere, for example by slightly rearranging the angle of a chair so that you are at right angles to rather than facing straight across from the person you are talking to. Where possible, avoid having the barrier of a desk or table between people – unless, of course, it's a round table discussion! Having a solid piece of furniture between you and your listener can create a psychological as well as a physical barrier between you.

Remember: you are trying to convey to your listener that you are someone worth listening to.

GAINING ATTENTION

This rule applies whether you are speaking to a crowded lecture room, pitching for converts to a political group or religion, meeting a new person at a party or speaking to your nearest and dearest about who is going to take the kids to the swimming pool. If you don't gain your listener's attention you risk them not hearing your message. Ways of gaining attention include:

Verbal attention grabbers
- Questions such as the typical conversation openers many of us use when meeting someone new, 'It's hot, isn't it?', 'Do you know many people here?', 'I couldn't help noticing the attractive jacket you're wearing. Where did you get it?', 'Did you see this TV programme/newspaper report/film or whatever?'.
- Exclamations such as 'Hey . . .', 'Hello!', 'Hi!', even simply, 'Listen!'.
- Telling an anecdote, story or account of something that happened to you or someone else; making a joke or funny remark.
- Giving a promise: for example if you are asking your teenage daughter to clear up her bedroom, 'If you clear up your bedroom now, we can go to McDonald's for a burger later on.'

Non-verbal attention grabbers
- Physical gestures such as waving, touching the arm of the person you wish to talk to, looking them straight in the eye, going up to the person you want to speak to.
- Clothing. For example, wearing something eye-catching if you are going to a party, speaking in public, appearing on TV.
- Tone of voice. Speaking more loudly or softly than normal, laughing, crying, shaking or expressing your emotions physically (this is usually involuntary).

Physical distance
- How close should you stand or are you standing to the person you are talking to and how does that distance affect your message? You will need to use different strategies if you are speaking from a rostrum to those you will use if you are standing next to someone in a public place or sitting across from them in a restaurant. Think about your distance before deciding how to put across your message. If you want to declare your love to your current boyfriend/girlfriend should you go up close and whisper in his/her ear? Shout or wave from across a room? Announce it on the radio? Put a Valentine's Day notice in the paper?

Remember: make sure you have your listener's attention before you begin to speak.

PAVING THE WAY FOR WHAT YOU ARE GOING TO SAY

Sometimes you may want to say something that is shocking or unexpected, in which case you will usually need to prepare your listener. For example, if you want to talk to your partner about selling the house and using the proceeds to fund opening a bar on the Greek island you went to on holiday last year, it will pay to think carefully about how to prepare him or her for this suggestion. If you are trying to persuade someone about something they may feel reluctant about, it's worthwhile thinking about how you might emphasise the benefits they stand to gain from it. If you are the bearer of bad news, emphasise the importance of what you have to say when you try to gain your listener's attention.

Some ways to prepare your listener:

- Come to the point clearly and quickly and say what you want to say.
- Offer a carrot. Tell your listener what s/he might gain as a result of what you are suggesting. For example 'If we go and live in Corfu you'll be able to give up working for the council and enjoy a sunny climate for more months of the year.'

- Check that your listener is ready and willing to listen to what you have to say. If you have to tell your teenage son he has failed all his 'A' levels don't start to do so while he's glued to a football match on the TV.
- Warn your listener of the importance of what you have to say. For example if you have to tell one of your employees that you are making them redundant help prepare them by saying something like, 'There's something important I have to tell you that will probably come as a shock.'
- Ask a question to arouse their curiosity. If you've just mortgaged your life savings for that bar in Greece: 'Guess what I did today?'

PUTTING YOUR MESSAGE ACROSS

Obvious as it may seem, one of the keys to good communication is to be clear about what you want to say. If you aren't and you don't get your message across, inevitably you will fail to get what you want because the person you are trying to get something from fails to pick up the point you are trying to put across.

One of the simplest yet least used ways, of getting what you want is quite simply to ask for it. This applies to all sorts of things that you might want, from a job, to a promotion, an engagement ring or even a new baby. If you do pluck up the courage to ask in a straightforward way you may be surprised. Kate, 19, who wants to be a theatre designer had spent a year after school getting some work experience in the theatre. She had done various jobs – costume assistant, assistant stage manager, general dogsbody and so on – and was just beginning to earn some money for her labours. One day she was asked to attend an interview for a job as assistant stage manager for a new production. At the interview she said, 'I don't actually want to be assistant stage manager but I would like to be assistant set designer.' Although the company didn't actually have such a post they created one for her – and she got paid! The lesson is clear: you'll never get what you want if you are afraid to ask for it.

NEVER ASSUME

It's often easy to assume (incorrectly) that the other person knows what you are thinking and to work yourself up into a lather because you feel your wishes are being ignored when simply making them plain would at least enable you to start negotiations. It also pays to be aware of the 'hidden agenda' you may have but your partner or the person you are speaking to isn't aware of. For instance, you assume that getting married means starting a family, he thought that it meant waiting for a few years until you had a house and a car. You assume that being given a deadline of such and such a date for a piece of work means you can overrun by a few days/hours, your boss assumes that you will deliver the work on the dot. Making clear your expectations by laying them on the table and discussing them can avoid a good deal of confusion and crossed messages.

MAKING SURE YOUR MESSAGE GETS ACROSS

Consider the following:

- Speak audibly enough for your message to be heard: whether it's whispering in your partner's ear, 'I want to leave this party now,' or asking in a crowded shop for a discount on something you are buying, make sure that the person you are speaking to is able to hear you.
- Use your voice. Pick up a few tips from actors who vary the pitch, tone and volume of their voices to keep the audience's attention and interest. If you speak in a dull monotone your listener can be forgiven for switching off and not listening
- Keep an eye out for signs that the other person hasn't understood what you are saying or is not interested, and either try to explain things more clearly or introduce a new fact that will engage the other person's interest. For example, if your bank manager seems bored by your plan to market your paintings,

suggest holding an exhibition in the bank. Other ways of reviving the other person's interest include making an arresting statement or gesture (a conversation stopper!), changing your body language, speaking more loudly or quietly, altering the emotional tone of the conversation (by getting angry, making a joke, telling someone about a particularly sad or funny incident) and so on.

- Give your listener the opportunity to ask questions or for clarification. Have some answers to likely questions ready.
- Summarise what you are saying to help the other person to understand. For example, 'So what I'm saying is if you manage to get production up by 90% in the next month, you'll be in for a promotion.'
- Stay on your listener's side. Talk to your listener and not at him or her. In other words, don't lecture, and try to see his or her point of view
- Be prepared to change tactics if you don't appear to be getting anywhere. If you feel that your message isn't getting across, you may need to think again. Perhaps the person you are speaking to is preoccupied, perhaps either or both of you are tired, upset or simply bored. In such cases, either fix a later time to talk about the matter in hand, suggest a short break, or change the way you are trying to get your message across, bearing in mind the points already mentioned.

BRINGING CONVERSATIONS TO AN END

We've all been stuck for hours on the 'phone to a friend who endlessly repeats his or her problems over and over again or in a business meeting that overruns by hours. Often when a conversation or meeting goes round and round it is simply a matter of what has to be said having been said but no one knowing how to end it. In such situations, it can help to have a few tricks up your sleeve for bringing the conversation to a close. Think about the following ideas:

- Ask the other person to do something or react to what has been discussed in some way. This can be a verbal reaction, or it can be something he or she has to go and do. 'So Ms Smith, you'll write me a report on . . .'; 'What do you think about what we've been discussing, John?'
- Suggest some ways to proceed further. For example, 'So I think we're all agreed that we need to lobby the Houses of Parliament'; 'We need to get a list of MPs who would be interested in . . .'
- Summarise what you have achieved in this particular conversation. For example, to the friend who always expects you to look after the children, 'So we're agreed that you'll do the school run every other day.'
- Indicate that you have finished or are about to finish either in words – 'So that just about winds up our meeting Mr Brown' – or non-verbally, by starting to tidy away your papers, put away your pen, stand up, put your coat on . . .
- Thank the person for their time, and arrange to meet again. If you are hosting a meeting for example, 'Well thank you everyone for coming and the next meeting is on 24th July.' The same can apply on social occasions too, 'It's been lovely seeing you again, Jane, see you next Saturday.'

FOLLOW UP

Sometimes you may need to follow up what has been agreed or discussed to make sure something gets done, to stay in touch or simply to maintain your relationship with someone. In work situations, for example, you might want to make a follow-up 'phone call or send a written memo summarising the main points and any action that has to be taken. In social situations you can be more informal, 'I'll ring you on Wednesday to see how you got on talking to Graham'; 'I'll get back to you on whether I can make Monday.'

ARE YOU A GOOD LISTENER?

Just as there are ways we can get in tune with other people through the way we communicate, there are also barriers which prevent us from getting close to people and understanding them better. Check out the following characters. Are there any you recognise – or worse still are you one of them yourself?

- **Know it all Norman**. He feels inferior to everyone else, so he is constantly trying to demonstrate his superiority by appearing better than the person he is talking to. Norman always knows better than you – whether you are discussing the latest restaurant or the best way to put a business plan into practice. If you suggest something Norman is the first to pour cold water on your suggestion – and substitute some (better) one of his own.
- **Interrupting Irene**. Irene is so busy thinking about what she has to say that she never listens to what you are saying. She constantly butts in with her own ideas and suggestions and never lets you finish what you are saying.
- **Rambling Rosie**. Rosie never stops talking: she simply rambles on from one sentence to the next without a break. Her conversations are boring and long and full of meaningless words and phrases which she uses to fill in the gaps, just so long as she never needs to stop rambling. She talks to keep your attention or simply to avoid you noticing that she doesn't really have anything to say at all.
- **I'm Igor**. Ego-on-legs Igor never stops talking about himself. Deep down, he suspects that he isn't actually all that big a deal, so just to make sure that you never notice he keeps the conversation firmly focused on number 1. Every conversation you start soon comes back to what Igor does and what Igor thinks.
- **Monotonous Mary**. Mary, too, never stops talking but unlike Rosie she talks to herself. She answers her own questions, laughs at her own jokes, and never listens to anybody else. In Mary's monotonous monologues there's no room for anyone else – besides Mary.

LEARNING TO LISTEN MORE EFFECTIVELY

Good listening is an art. It is more than simply the physical act of hearing with your ears or 'not speaking'. It is an active process of attending and responding to what the person you are speaking to has to say.

People who know how to listen are better at getting what they want because they are alert to the messages other people are trying to put across. Yet research shows that three-quarters of what we say to each other is ignored, misunderstood or forgotten.

To listen effectively you need to develop the following skills:

- Want to listen. If you are bored, tired, uninterested or distracted by something else you will not listen effectively and it will show. As a result the other person may rush what they want to say or not say it at all.
- Make judicious use of silence and questions to show that you are listening and to get more information.
- Encourage the other person to talk by repeating or rephrasing what the person you are talking to has said. This makes your partner feel heard and ensures that you have heard correctly and received the correct message.
- Keep an open mind. Don't judge what the other person is saying until you have heard him or her out.
- Take time to think about what the person has said and how you will respond to it. Don't jump in immediately with your comments or interrupt the other person's flow.
- Be willing to look behind what is being said to see whether there is an underlying message or issue. If there is, be prepared to probe and encourage the person to talk about what is really bothering them. For example, 'It seems to me that what you are really saying is . . .'; 'Am I right in thinking that what you are really bothered about is . . .?'; 'The real problem seems to be . . .'
- Be attentive to what the person is saying. It is easy to switch off because you are bored or because you disagree with what the

person is saying. Be aware of when you are doing this and make an effort to re-engage your attention.
- Try to avoid getting hung up on minor points of detail and so miss the main point. Make an effort to understand the main issue in question and if necessary ask for clarification. For example, 'So what you are saying is . . .'; 'Do I understand you to be saying . . . ?'; 'What exactly do you mean?'; 'So, the main issue is . . .!'
- Concentrate on what the person you are talking to is saying. Try to switch off your personal preoccupations and worries when you are talking to someone and pay attention to what they are saying. If you are undergoing a personal crisis and you really can't switch your mind away from it, suggest that you talk at a later date.
- Avoid trying to impose your own agenda on the conversation. Give a fair hearing to what the person you are talking to is saying and don't try to win them over to your argument without first listening to what they have to say.

GETTING CLOSE

Good communication is also important in moving relationships on at work, at home or in social situations. There are many ways of getting close. One very simple way is to get in tune physically with the people you meet. Have you ever noticed how two friends or people who are getting on well together tend to sit in the same way, hold themselves in the same way and adopt similar expressions? In close, loving relationships, partners sometimes even breathe in unison and as a result their heart beats (controlled by the autonomic nervous system) start to beat at the same pace – literally two hearts beating as one.

Consciously mirroring someone's body language can help you get closer to someone in your personal relationships with your partner, friends and relatives. In your work and social relationships, it can help other people to feel comfortable in your presence and that you are on their side. Next time you are talking to someone, try subtly mirroring the way they sit and their gestures and see how much better your conversation goes.

Opening up about yourself, what psychologists call self-disclosure, is another way of getting close to someone. Being willing to talk openly and honestly about yourself is the only way other people can really get to know and trust you. Talking about yourself, your ideas, your feelings and emotions, is one way of getting to know someone better and moving a relationship on – provided you pick your moment carefully. For example, it would hardly be appropriate to start spilling your deepest feelings about your partner's affair with his secretary when you are in the middle of asking your bank manager for a loan to start a new business. Many of us use self-disclosure, quite unconsciously of course, when we make friends. For example you go out to a wine bar for a business meeting and end up staying way after the meeting has finished talking about your delight or fears about your forthcoming wedding, children or whatever; your colleague responds with how he felt in similar situations – and hey presto, your colleague becomes your friend.

Most of us have fears about whether we are acceptable and whether other people like us. Talking about yourself is one way of dispelling such fears and reassuring other people that you accept them for who they are. Used carefully and appropriately, there are few more powerful ways of creating closeness and intimacy than self-disclosure.

TALKING ABOUT WHAT YOU WANT ROUND UP

Now you know how to communicate with other people you are another step further to getting what you want. In the next chapter we are going to look at some of the barriers – both self-imposed and imposed by other people – that may stand in the way of getting what you want. But first let's just check on what you have learnt in this chapter. Tick the boxes you agree with.

- [ ] I know what I want to say and feel able to put it across clearly and effectively.
- [ ] I am aware of the part body language plays in what I say and what other people say to me.

> - ☐ I am able to choose the most appropriate way of saying what I want to say.
> - ☐ I am sensitive to what the person I am talking to is saying to me and aware of their body language.
> - ☐ I am confident that I am able to establish and maintain relationships with the people I want.

Now let's have a look at some of the things that might be stopping you from getting what you want and some ways to avoid them.

CHAPTER SEVEN
AVOIDING THE TRIP WIRES

The process of making choices, implementing decisions and turning your dreams into reality doesn't always run smoothly, however motivated you are and however efficiently you put your plans into action. Everyone who ever achieves anything encounters some setbacks on the road to what they want – and you are no exception. Some of the things that are stopping you may be throwbacks from your past – outworn ideas or beliefs about yourself – whose time has come to be ditched. Other setbacks may simply reflect the fact that the course you have chosen is hard. In this case, apply yourself to solving your problems (you'll find some hints in this chapter) – and congratulate yourself when you do so.

Sometimes the barriers will be clear to you. At other times you may simply feel 'stuck' and not know what to do about it. This chapter is about identifying the barriers that are holding you back and bringing them into the open so you can tackle them.

WHAT'S HOLDING YOU BACK?

Most barriers fall into one of two types:

> 1. Those that come from the outside – from other people, events or circumstances beyond your control

> 2. Those that come from inside you – some of these may have originated outside you, from your parents, your teachers, religious leaders and others, but you have made them part of your own thinking. Others may be a result of your individual outlook on life, especially your optimism or pessimism

Let's look at each of these in turn and see what you can do about them.

BARRIERS IMPOSED BY EVENTS, CIRCUMSTANCES OR OTHER PEOPLE

Some of the setbacks you encounter may be totally out of your control: the computer breaking down as you are writing up the annual report, your mother dying when you are about to sit an important exam. The best you can hope for is to do some damage limitation, accept what has happened, and proceed as best you can. Such events and circumstances are the subject of my other book, *The Survivor Personality*.

Other barriers may be imposed by the important people in your life. Have a look at the following list and tick which statements apply to you:

> - My partner doesn't want me to ....
> - Whenever I try to change it seems to upset other people in my life
> - My family complain when I try to ....
> - The rest of my family aren't ambitious so it's hard for me to ....
>
>   Add any other statements that apply to you ....

Any form of change may be threatening to those you care for: your parents, your children, your partner, your friends. Often such people resist change because they fear losing something – your friendship, partnership, love . . . At other times they may fear their own position is threatened by the changes you are making. For example, if your partner has always been the breadwinner and made the rules in your household he may fear losing his status if you get a job. Sometimes the fear arises from a threat to the power balance that is operating in a particular relationship. If you have always been there to cook your children's dinner and iron their clothes, they may fear you won't be there for them if you take a job. In each of these cases, you need to identify what they feel they will lose and then point out the ways in which they will gain. For example, 'If I take a job we'll be able to buy a second car'; 'If I give up my job we'll be able to spend more time together.' You will be more likely to succeed in allaying the fears of those around you if you are able to make an appeal to the things you know they value. For example, if one of your partner's main values is 'having fun', play up the potential for fun time that your taking a job will create — more holidays, meals out, whatever he thinks of as 'fun' activities. But before you blame your failure to achieve what you want entirely on other people, it's worth pointing out that you yourself may have doubts about how the changes you are planning to make will affect your life. For example, 'Will I have as much time for my partner/children/friends if I . . .?'; 'How will the changes I plan to make affect my role in my family and social circle?' Confronting your fears openly and honestly and thinking about ways in which you might deal with them can show them up for the insubstantial creatures they really are.

ARE YOU MAKING EXCUSES?

Some of the barriers you may encounter are little more than 'excuses' you have imposed upon yourself, perhaps to protect yourself from fear of failure. As such they are often relatively simple to deal with — once you have exposed them for what they are. Do you recognise any of these?

- 'I don't have the time'
  Go on, admit it, however much you have on your plate, you still find time to do the things you really want to do. This book is designed for people who are leading busy lives. It's not necessarily true that the more time you give to a project the better the results, since we all know work expands to fit the time available. In Chapter Four you learnt how to organise your time so as to make more time for the things you want to do. But at the

end of the day if you can't find the time for something you say you want to do, perhaps you should ask yourself, 'How much do I really want to do it?'

- 'I can't afford it'
  The same comments apply to money, as you discovered in Chapter Five. It may be a question of spending less, finding ways to create more, or both. But if you really and truly want to do something, then you will usually find the wherewithal.
- 'I can't change the habits of a lifetime'
  You can – if you really want to! In this case, your problem could be fear of what the changes you are proposing to make will lead to. For one thing is guaranteed, once you start to change you will find the world changes too – your job, your relationships, your interests and beliefs. It's not surprising if you find the prospect scary. Fear of change is only natural. It is only by confronting your fears and anxieties and bringing them out into the open that you can conquer them. As US author Susan Jeffers says in her very encouraging book, *Feel the Fear And Do*, 'Remember: you always have a choice, even if you don't choose to take it.'

INTERNAL BARRIERS

Far more difficult to deal with than any of the above are the deeper barriers you impose upon yourself. Some of these may have come originally from the world outside – from your particular culture. Have a look at the following list and tick the statements that you recognise:

> - People of my class/colour/education/gender don't .....
> - Women should put relationships before work.
> - Men should put work before family.
>
> Add any other social pressures you are aware of that you feel are stopping you from achieving your goals.

All these statements reflect cultural ideas about the way we should be. If what you want involves breaking new ground – the first woman in your social group, the first black person, the first young/old person to do a certain thing – you may well come up against barriers, both from the outside and from the messages you have absorbed about what it is possible/desirable for someone from your social/cultural/age group to do. If you can understand and confront these social pressures and have the confidence to go for what you want, you'll discover the special exhilaration that comes from being a trail-blazer. And once the barriers are down it becomes that bit easier for the next person to get across, and the one after, and the one after that . . . So the stream becomes a tide – and that's how the world changes.

WHO'S PULLING YOUR STRINGS?

Many psychologists describe our personality structure as having three parts:

- The Parent
- The Adult
- The Child

Many of the negative messages that cripple our ability to get what we want come from the 'Parent' parts of our personality and have often been absorbed from our real parents. For example:

'You'll never make it as a fashion designer, you can't draw to save your life.'

'What makes you think you can have a happy marriage? All men are monsters.'

'You'll never have the staying power to get fit, you've never stuck to anything in your life.'

Becoming aware of these messages and switching on the mature, 'Adult' part of your personality will help you combat them. For example:

'Sure, I'll be able to cope with teaching that course. I've always been interested in the subject and I'm convinced I can put my enthusiasm across.'

'If I start training now I'll be fit to run the marathon next year.'

Each one of us also has an inner 'Child', which provides us with the initial desire and enthusiasm to do something:

'Hey, why don't I give up my job and sail round the world — it's something I've always wanted to do.'

Ideally, all three aspects of our personality structure would be perfectly integrated. However, all too often one particular part — usually the Child or Parent — dominates or the different parts are at war. This is one of the main reasons some of us fail to get what we want. Let's look at an example. You have a thought: 'I'd like to give up my job and spend the summer in Greece.' (Child.) Immediately, your Parent jumps in, 'How can you consider such a thing? You are so irresponsible. What will you live on? You'll never get another job when you get back.' While these two are battling it out the Adult part of your personality doesn't get a look in. If you can switch it on you might think, 'Well, that could be possible. You could contact your friend in Athens and find out if he knows any restaurant owners who are looking for staff. And if you use some of your savings and set up some project work for later in the year there should be no problems when you get back.'

It's up to you to become aware of who is pulling your strings so you can allow the three parts of your personality to work with rather than against each other. In the rest of the book, you'll find plenty of ideas to help you.

BREAK FREE FROM YOUR PAST

Getting what you want, then, involves breaking free from your past, letting go of old messages and moving forward into a future that is of your own choosing. But just to remind yourself look at the following Bill of Rights based on a list of 'freedoms' devised by US psychologist Virginia Satir. Write them down on a card and stick them above your desk, in your wallet, on the fridge door, inside your wardrobe, or anywhere where you will see them regularly. Next time you feel you have lost sight of where you are going read them:

I have the freedom to:

1. See and hear what is here, instead of what should be, was or will be

2. Say what I feel and think, instead of what you imagine I should feel and think

3. Feel what I feel, instead of what I ought to feel

4. Ask for what I want, instead of always waiting to be given permission

5. Take risks on my own behalf, instead of choosing to be 'secure' and not to rock the boat

SAY GOODBYE TO THE LOSER MENTALITY

Many of us create a lot of stress for ourselves by the way we think. One of the main differences between winners, people who get where they want to be and cope successfully with setbacks, and losers, those who don't, is quite simply their thinking style.

Have a look at the following list and tick any of those that apply to you:

- I'm not sure I can get what I want because I've tried before and failed.
- I always start to make changes with enthusiasm but I soon lose heart.
- If I fail everyone will see I'm a fraud/that my previous success was a fluke.
- I feel guilty if I spend time on myself.

> - Change makes me feel miserable and depressed.
> - I'll never be able to get what I want as quickly as I want to.
> - If I don't succeed in everything I do I'm a worthless person.

All these are reflections of an attitude to life known as the loser mentality, a habit of negative thinking, which you may have developed in childhood.

It was Shakespeare's Hamlet who said, 'There is nothing either good or bad but thinking makes it so . . .' In other words, the thoughts in our minds can hold us back or propel us forward. Psychologists have come up with several characteristic ways in which people with the loser mentality think.

- Losers impose over-rigid standards
  Losers are constantly tuned into those old messages from the past saying that they must be perfect and never fail. Such perfectionism inevitably leads to intolerance when they suffer a setback. If the loser is invited to a job interview s/he thinks: 'If I fail this interview it proves I'm completely useless.' The winner thinks, 'If I don't get this particular job there will be others and it's good practice going to the interview.'
- Losers exaggerate setbacks
  Instead of viewing something that goes wrong as a temporary blip, losers blow it up out of all proportion. As a result, they see it as the worst possible thing that could happen. The experts call this 'catastrophising'. If a loser puts on unwanted weight s/he thinks, 'I've put on over a stone since the summer, I can't stand it.' By contrast, the winner thinks, 'OK, so I have put some weight on, but if I start exercising and eating sensibly now it won't take me long to lose it.'
- Losers blame themselves for things that go wrong
  If you are in a losing frame of mind and have fallen out with your new boyfriend you think, 'It was all my fault, if I hadn't turned up late at the restaurant he wouldn't have been in a bad temper and then we wouldn't have had that argument. How can anyone

like me expect ever to have a boyfriend?' The winner might think, 'He was obviously feeling edgy in the first place and my arriving late can't have helped, but who cares, there are plenty more men out there.'

'The optimist thinks that this may be one of the best days ever. The pessimist fears that the optimist might be right.' If your losing outlook is holding you back, now is the time to start thinking like a winner. But first, as always, you must gather some information about where you are now. Do the following quiz to see if you think like a loser or a winner. Tick the ones that apply to you:

1. a) I hardly ever expect things to go my way.

   b) I usually expect things to turn out well for me.

2. a) I feel powerless to change my life.

   b) I am in control of my own life.

3. a) I feel there's little point in trying to change things.

   b) If I don't like the way things are, I look at ways of trying to change them.

4. a) I often feel depressed and apathetic.

   b) I usually feel positive and full of energy.

5. a) I feel that life is passing me by.

   b) I feel I get the most out of life.

6. a) I feel worthless compared with people who are more successful than me.

   b) I feel equal to other people.

7. a) I often feel worthless and insignificant compared with my friends.

   b) I value my friends and their differences from me.

8. a) I often feel misunderstood by other people.

   b) I understand myself and feel confident that I can communicate who I am to other people.

9. a) I often feel embarrassed and awkward by the way I behave with other people.

   b) I usually feel confident in my dealings with other people.

10. a) I often feel alone and unloved.

    b) I feel loved and appreciated by the people who mean a lot to me.

11. a) If something goes wrong I usually give up trying to reach my goal.

    b) If something goes wrong I concentrate on dealing with it and if necessary let other things slide a little.

12. a) I often feel guilty about things that go wrong.

    b) I usually try to learn from things that have gone wrong.

13. a) When something bad happens to me I tend to feel overwhelmed.

    b) When something bad happens I try to find something good in what is happening.

14. a) I usually feel depressed when something goes wrong.

    b) I can usually see the funny side of most situations.

15. a) When I am having to cope with a difficult situation I tend to bottle up my emotions and try to deal with it on my own.

    b) When I am having to cope with a difficult situation I know who I can turn to for help and support.

16. a) When faced with a problem I tend to drink more/smoke more/take drugs to help me deal with it.

    b) When facing a situation or a problem I try to come up with a strategy of how to deal with it.

17. a) Faced with a problem I often find it hard to believe it has happened or say it isn't real.

    b) Faced with a problem I usually face up to it and try hard to prevent other things from interfering with my efforts to deal with it.

How did you get on? No prizes for guessing which answers are those of winners (b's) and those of losers (a's). Ever since the 1950s when the US psychologist Norman Vincent Peale developed the theory of positive thinking – the idea that being confident and upbeat can actually help you to achieve more – it's been known that thinking winning thoughts can help you to get what you want. Being positive, thinking like a winner, allows you to develop and maintain your confidence in yourself and gives you the courage to confront and overcome obstacles. There's now a huge amount of psychological research to suggest that if you expect to succeed you stand a better chance of actually doing so, because you will view setbacks as something to be worked at and overcome. On the other hand, if you expect to fail you are more likely to reduce your efforts and give up on your goals in the face of obstacles.

Winners

- Possess a zest for life – an energetic approach towards whatever life throws up

- Have confidence – a positive outlook

- Are resourceful – take a creative attitude towards problem-solving

- Show flexibility – the willingness to take risks and make changes

> **Losers**
> - Are lacking in energy and enthusiasm
> - Have low self-confidence – a negative outlook
> - Only see one way of solving problems – may retreat into sleep or drink or other addictions
> - Are rigid – unwilling to take risks and make changes

DEVELOPING WINNING STRATEGIES

There's also a lot of evidence to suggest that optimists, or winners, actually use different coping strategies from pessimists. In particular, if you believe deep down that 'things will work out' you are more likely to focus on problems and work out constructive ways to deal with obstacles and setbacks. At the same time, when faced with a situation that is unchangeable, if you are an optimist you are more likely to accept the reality of your problems rather than wishing them away.

If you have a pessimistic outlook, on the other hand, you will tend to distance yourself from stressful situations or dwell on distressing emotions such as anger, sorrow and regret, which drag you down and prevent you from moving on or overcoming difficulties. If you are pessimistic about life where a situation is unavoidable, you continue to deny that it has happened or that you can attempt to escape. To give an example: if you are basically of an optimistic nature and you develop difficulties in your relationship you are more likely to sit down with your partner, go and see a counsellor or work out other strategies for tackling your problems. If this doesn't work out the optimist is more likely to accept that the situation can't be saved and move on. On the other hand if you are a pessimist you may be more likely to seek ways to escape the situation you find yourself in. Avoidance tactics may include things like having an affair, taking refuge in overeating, drinking, smoking, sleeping, watching TV or going to the movies, and escaping into daydreams or fantasies. The danger is that such strategies, tempting though they are, actually do nothing to change the situation and can sometimes make it worse. In the long run, refusing to face up to the reality may make you stay in a hopeless relationship for longer and take longer to get over it.

In other words, optimists are more likely to be active in the face of distressing events and less likely to seek escape or dwell on their distress. Simply being active and using effective coping strategies makes you feel in control. There's another bonus too. Several research studies have shown that optimism is linked to physical health and well-being.

IS PESSIMISM ALWAYS A BAD THING?

Surprisingly, given the advantages of developing an optimistic outlook, there are some circumstances in which pessimism pays off. In the past few years, experts have identified a style of coping which they describe as 'defensive pessimism'. If you are a defensive pessimist, you may anticipate that you will do badly at something, even though you have always done well before, and therefore increase your effort to try and ensure that you do well. Defensive pessimism helps to protect you against disappointment and failure; also, worrying about the possibility of failing may actually goad you into action. So in some circumstances pessimism can actually help you to succeed, but, and it's a big 'but', it tends to work best in the short term. For example, in one piece of US research, first-year college students who were defensive pessimists did as well as optimists in their first year, but as time went on the strategy proved less effective, so that by their final year they performed less well and were less satisfied with their lives than optimistic students.

LOSER TO WINNER

The good news is that even if you think like a loser now, you can learn to think like a winner. And one of the most effective ways is simply to transform your losing thoughts by turning them around. Let's look at an example:

- *Sally had just finished a journalism course and was desperate to get a job on a magazine. She had applied for a post on a particular magazine, and was sent a set of exercises to do to enable the employers to select who they wanted to interview. Unfortunately, the post was slow, it was a Bank Holiday and the material didn't arrive until the day before it was due to be sent back. The next day Sally had to work in another office. A stressful situation.*

Let's examine the thoughts that could transform this situation in Sally's mind into a losing one. The process begins with a want – Sally's desire to get a job on the magazine. Sally's losing thoughts transform the desire into a demand – 'I must get this job otherwise I'm a total failure' – and this immediately places her under pressure. Next, she becomes aware of the deadline and makes herself even more miserable by thinking, 'I'll never get these exercises done in the time I've got and then they'll realise how useless I am.'

Now let's see how Sally could transform her losing thoughts into winning ones, and so boost not only her chances of getting the job but also her self-esteem. First of all, her desire for the job. 'Yes, I would like a job on this magazine, but if I don't get it then other jobs will come up that I can apply for. I'm well-qualified and I know I can do the work, so sooner or later I will get a job on a magazine.' Next the deadline, 'The post was late so I'll ring up and ask if I can have an extra day to do the exercises. That way I show myself as someone who takes her responsibilities seriously.' By adopting this approach, by the time Sally has to go for the interview she is feeling confident and relaxed and performs her best.

Incidentally this example is based on a real-life person – and yes, she did get the job!

TRANSFORMING YOUR LOSING THOUGHTS

Now it's time for you to learn to stop your losing thoughts in their tracks. You will need a notebook and a pencil.

> Over the next few days write down any incidents where you notice you are thinking or reacting like a loser. Note your emotions and physical feelings. Losing thoughts tend to be accompanied by emotions of depression, anxiety and

stress together with all the physical accompaniments of these such as a racing heart, dry mouth, clenched stomach, tense shoulders and so on. It's not always easy to identify your own habits of losing thinking, simply because they are so automatic, so let your friends, colleagues or partner in on the act, and ask them to point out examples.

Now you have pinpointed your losing thoughts you can begin to challenge them. Each time you catch yourself reacting like a loser STOP! and do the following:

Challenge your musts, shoulds and oughts

Q. 'Why must I succeed at everything I attempt and never have any worries or upsets?'

A. 'I don't have to succeed even though I would like to do so. I have to experience worries and upsets because that is part of everyday life. It's a pity – but there it is.'

Challenge your tendency to exaggerate

Q. 'Where is the evidence that I can't stand such and such?'

A. 'Nowhere. I won't die because of what has happened and I can be happy in spite of it. It is not horrible, but only bearably painful.'

Challenge your feelings of worthlessness

Q. 'Am I an inadequate, worthless person because such and such happened?'

A. 'No, I may well have not handled this particular situation as well as I could, but that doesn't make me totally worthless (or good), just a fallible human being who is doing my best to cope with a difficult situation.'

From now on, every time you face a difficult situation write it down in your notebook and try to see the positive aspects of it. For example:

- Situation: You got pregnant just as you were about to take your first job.
- Losing thought: That's it, my career's ruined, I'll be stuck in dead-end jobs for the rest of my life. I'm a totally worthless person.
- Winning thought: That's great. Now I will have a child to care for and love. Having a child at my age while I'm at the peak of my health and strength is wonderful. What's more, I've got plenty of time to work out what I want to do and concentrate on my career.

You see by changing your losing thoughts to winning ones you immediately feel more in control. And that is tremendously empowering. Instead of seeing yourself as the victim of circumstance, you give yourself choices.

So next time you face a period of stress try thinking: 'Yes, I am under a lot of stress right now, but there's not much I can do about a lot of it. I don't have to get rid of the stress and I can lead a reasonable happy life even if my problems continue.'

The words you use can make you a winner or a loser.

LOSER	WINNER
- I can't	- I won't
- I should	- I could
- It's not my fault	- I'm responsible
- It's a problem	- It's a challenge
- I hope	- I know
- If only	- Next time
- What am I going to do?	- I can deal with this
- It's a catastrophe	- It's a chance to learn

Some other ways to get on a winning wicket:

- Make a plan of action. Think about what you can do to try and overcome obstacles and do your best to follow it. If your plan doesn't work out after a period of time think out some new options.
- Talk to other people about how you are feeling and express your emotions but try to avoid getting bogged down in them. Dwelling on negative emotions can actually prevent you from tackling your problems constructively.
- Ask other people for their advice on how they coped in similar situations and see whether any of their coping strategies might work for you. As before, concentrate on active coping rather than sinking into misery or attempting to escape the situation.
- See the opportunities for growth and change in stressful experiences. For example 'I may have lost my job, but at least I don't have to spend three hours travelling on the Underground every day and now I have all the time in the world to write my novel/travel the world/make a film . . .'
- Learn to laugh. Many things that happen to us are not at all funny but it's often possible to find the humour in even the blackest situation. Psychological research shows that being able to laugh can do much to lighten your mood and make it easier to maintain an optimistic outlook.

AVOIDING THE TRIP WIRES ROUND UP

So now you have defined the barriers that are holding you back from getting what you want. In the next part of the book we'll be looking at how to get what you want in specific situations and applying the knowledge that you have gained by working your way through the previous sections.

But, before we move on, let's check you have taken on board what you have read in this chapter. Tick the following:

> - [ ] Can you identify the barriers that have stopped you getting what you want in the past?
> - [ ] Can you identify why other people may be making life difficult for you?
> - [ ] Are you aware of the different parts of your personality and how they may be aiding you or holding you back?
> - [ ] Are you confident that you can transform your losing thoughts to winning ones?

Yes? Then you're ready to take the next step – but give yourself time and be patient. Getting what you want involves changes in the way you think and feel and in what you do and this can sometimes be disturbing to you and other people. And remember you already started to get what you want when you picked up this book.

PART TWO
MAKING THINGS HAPPEN

INTRODUCTION

In Part One you learned about a basic plan for turning your dreams into reality. In Part Two, you will put that plan into action in five main areas of your life.

- Your work
- Your relationships
- Your appearance
- Your health and longevity
- Your personal growth

I have chosen to concentrate on these areas, because I believe that most of the things that we want fall into them. However, the precise things you want may not be dealt with here. Don't worry. The plan you have learn can be applied to any of your dreams. In this part of the book you will become proficient at doing just that, so that whatever you decide you want in life you have the mental, physical and spiritual resources you need to go for it. Never doubt that:

- You can create the time
- You can create the money
- You can find the people
- You can do what you want

Now let's get going.

CHAPTER EIGHT
GETTING THE WORK YOU WANT

Time was when people left school, college or university to get a 'proper' job with good pay, regular holidays, an annual works outing and at the end of it a golden handshake or even a pension. Such a job offered security, status and a place in the world. Those times have gone: the world of work has undergone a revolution, and our whole lives are changing with it. Hardly any of us these days can expect to spend the whole of our lives in one job. In fact, today most people can expect to change job or career several times. This can be an unsettling thought, but the new way of working can be a ticket to a freer, more fulfilling life.

In this chapter you will learn how to get work that satisfies and fulfils you whether you are looking for a job for the first time, changing career or returning to work after a career break. You will learn whether you are suited to start up your own business. And you will learn how to check that the job you are doing is still suited to your needs. In so doing, don't forget to apply the five-step plan for turning your dreams into reality that you read about in Part One.

> Step one: Get in touch with your dream
>
> Step two: Research your dream
>
> Step three: Think out your plan of action

> Step four: Put your plan into action
>
> Step five: Check your progress

If you haven't ever worked or have spent some time having a career break, you may feel equally at sea. 'I don't have any skills. I can't do anything,' you wail. Well, now I'm going to prove to you that simply by living your life so far you have acquired a vast range of skills, talents and abilities, which can be put to use in finding a job or work that is right for you.

WHO ARE YOU?

The first thing to do is to identify the sorts of things you like to do which make you who you are. The work universe is a fascinating and complex one that contains many different worlds. To find out where your main interests, abilities and talents lie, read through the next section and tick the statements that apply to you. You will need some time and a pen and notebook.

> **Are you a doer?**
> - I like fixing and repairing things
> - I like exercise, sport, and keeping fit
> - I enjoy using my hands
> - I like making things
> - I enjoy physical work
> - I enjoy driving a car
> - I enjoy using tools and machinery

If you have ticked many of these you are primarily a doer, or practical person. You feel happiest working with tools, objects, machinery or animals rather than with people or ideas. You prefer to solve problems by doing rather than thinking. The best jobs for you involve using your hands and your body. You enjoy the outdoor life and prefer to deal with concrete problems rather than abstract ones.

> **Are you a thinker?**
>
> - I like to understand things
> - I like to explore new ideas
> - I enjoy solving problems
> - I like to ask questions
> - I enjoy learning about new things

If you have ticked many of these you are a thinker, an ideas person. You are curious, independent, intellectual and may have a tendency to be inward-looking. You may be eccentric or unconventional. You enjoy thinking through intellectual problems and using your mental abilities to come up with solutions. The best jobs for you involve observing, learning, investigating, analysing and evaluating.

> **Are you a creator?**
>
> - I enjoy creative writing, drawing or painting, sculpture, pottery, composing music
> - I enjoy art exhibitions, the theatre, film
> - I like to be unconventional
> - I like to have beautiful objects around me
> - I like to use my imagination

If you have ticked many of these you are a creative person. You enjoy beauty, variety and using your imagination. You approach the world through your senses: the sights, sounds, colours, and textures of things around you. You may be unconventional, sensitive, independent, introspective. You dislike routine and are happiest in jobs where you can exercise your creativity, for example in the arts and media.

> Are you a people person?
> - I enjoy being with other people
> - I like to talk things over with people
> - I like helping people
> - I like teaching people
> - Who I am with is more important than where I am

If you have ticked many of these you are a people person. You are highly tuned into your feelings and those of others. You approach life through interacting with other people: sharing problems, leading, informing, teaching, helping, curing. When solving problems you focus on your gut reactions. You are happiest in jobs which involve you working closely with other people, for example teacher, healer, nurse, counsellor, therapist.

> Are you an administrator?
> - I prefer to be given clear instructions as to what to do
> - I enjoy carrying out things in detail
> - I prefer to have a regular routine
> - I enjoy working with numbers
> - I enjoy organising projects, ideas and people

If you have ticked many of these you are an administrator. You enjoy analysing, sorting, sifting through data or information. You are highly organised and enjoy the fine detail of jobs, and are happy following instructions laid down by other people. Jobs that would suit you may involve working with figures or where a close attention to detail is required such as library assistant, information manager, secretary, administrator.

> Are you an entrepreneur?
> - I like trying to persuade and influence people
> - I am energetic
> - I enjoy having people under me who do what I ask
> - I enjoy taking risks
> - I like taking decisions
> - I enjoy organising and inspiring people

If you have ticked many of these you are an entrepreneur. You like to work with people, influencing, persuading or performing. You also enjoy organising and managing. You are likely to be ambitious, extrovert, independent, logical and oozing with confidence and vitality. You believe variety is the spice of life. You enjoy the good life, an affluent lifestyle, power and money. You are a risk taker. Jobs that might suit you include being a performer, a director of a company or starting your own company.

What did you find out about yourself? Were you surprised? You should now have a clearer idea of the sorts of skills, abilities and talents you are best at and enjoy the most. This is important because it determines the sort of careers and jobs you are likely to find most satisfying – and, as we've already seen, doing something you enjoy is a huge boost to motivation. You may have found that your skills, talents and interests lie in more than one area. If so, ideally, you should look for a job that satisfies all the various parts of your personality – otherwise you may never be entirely happy with the job you are in. If that isn't possible it's worth thinking about other ways you may express the different sides of you. The next step is to narrow down your search. But first, let's have a look at what you can already do.

> Here are some ideas for things you can do in the areas you have identified:
>
> **Practical:** skilled trades, technical and service which involve physical co-ordination and strength. Jobs using machinery or understanding mechanical principles, exploiting natural resources.
>
> **Data:** Scientific and technical, involving an interest in how and why things work or happen, interest in discovering facts, analysis and problem solving.
>
> **Creative:** Visual and performing arts, design, writing.
>
> **People:** Education, social welfare jobs which involve advice and helping other people with problems.
>
> **Administrative:** Office and clerical work, public administration, security, interest in organising procedures by means of paperwork.
>
> **Enterprise:** Managerial, sales, financial and services which involve managing, leading, negotiating or promoting products.

YOU KNOW MORE THAN YOU THINK YOU DO

If you have never had a job, just lost one, are going back to work or simply thinking of a change, you may feel unconfident because you can't imagine what you can do. So now I am going to prove to you that you have more skills than you realise. You will need some time and a pen and notebook.

> Look back over your life and make a list of ten things you have done which you enjoyed and feel particularly proud of. The experiences you choose can be jobs you have had, voluntary work, roles you played such as captain of the

hockey team or chairperson of a voluntary group, things you did in your spare time, and accomplishments or achievements at home, school or work. They don't have to be big or 'important' experiences and it doesn't matter what you choose so long as it involved you doing something and it gave you a real sense of enjoyment and achievement. Here are some of my suggestions: the article I wrote which won an award; setting up my own business; giving birth to my two children; learning to dance salsa. Use them to trigger off your own ideas.

Your list:

- ....
- ....
- ....
- ....
- ....
- ....
- ....
- ....
- ....

Feeling pleased with yourself? You should be. The skills you have identified are what are called your transferable skills and, as such, you can use them in all sorts of different ways. Think about the things you have listed and what they tell you about you. After you have done this think about what you have discovered. For instance into what areas do your main skills, interests and abilities fall? Are there any areas in which you feel you have undeveloped skills and talents (ask a good friend, partner or colleague)? Do you prefer routine or do you like variety and change? Are you a planner or a risk-taker? A talker or a listener? Do you prefer working to a deadline, immediate results, or long-term projects? How important is money as a motivating factor? Where would you like to work? This country or abroad? Any particular area, town or city? What sort of working environment do you prefer? Outdoors, indoors? In a large organisation or firm, a small company, self-employed? Do you prefer to work in uniform, a suit, or casual clothes? Do you want to work on your own, with one other person, as a member of a team? Do you want to be a supervisor, boss or owner? What degree of responsibility do you want? Do you prefer initiating ideas or working on other people's ideas?

There are usually several recognised steps on the ladder for any type of work:

- Step 1: Unskilled and semi-skilled jobs

  Qualifications needed: few or none

- Step 2: Skilled practical and clerical jobs

  Qualifications needed: some passes at GCSE/S level

- Step 3: Supervisory and middle management, technician and some professional levels

  Qualifications needed: at least GCSE/S level (A–C/1–3) plus 'A'/'H' level passes and some further training

- Step 4: Professional and higher managerial level

  Qualifications needed: degree or diploma/extensive experience and high level of skills. Postgraduate training.

WHAT'S YOUR LINE?

The next step is to take a long hard look at your present job or situation and analyse it: what you like and dislike about it, what things are important to you about it, what things you would like to keep, what things you would like to change. First of all, in your notebook, list ten things you like about your present job/career/situation and ten things you would like to change. You are now ready to use all your research to help you decide the direction in which you would most like go.

YOUR ACTION PLAN

Now you know what you are looking for in terms of your work you are ready to go.

> Write down your own personal 'want' list to remind you what you are looking for:
> - I want to work (place, organisation)............................
> - I want to earn ....
> - I want this level of responsibility ....
> - I want my working conditions to be ....
> - I want a job that involves using these kinds of special knowledge ....
> - I want a job that involves these kinds of relationships with other people ....
> - I want a job in this kind of working environment ....
> - I want a job that involves using these transferable skills (list the skills you want to use in order of their importance for you) ....

By now you should be able to picture your dream job in great detail, which is great, because it means you are focusing on what you *want* to do. And that is the next step in turning your dreams into reality. Remember your 'dream job' from Section One? How does it fit with what you have now found out? Do you want to alter it at all? If so, now is the time to do so.

SETTING GOALS

Now, at last, you are ready to turn your dreams into reality. To do this, as we discovered in Part One, you need to set yourself some goals. This will help you stay focused on what you want to do, increase your motivation, and help you monitor how you are doing.

For example, say you have decided to run your own landscape gardening business. Your short-term goals may include doing a course in garden design, doing a course on how to run your own business, getting work with a local landscape gardener, finding ways to earn or borrow the money to finance your project. So let's get down to it. Remember: goals should be positive, active and specific.

My plan of action:

- My long-term aim is ....
- My first step is..

HOW WILL YOU GET THERE?

Once you have set your goals, you need to think about some of the specific resources you might need to get there. For example you might need to develop your skills and knowledge in particular ways, or get more information about what jobs are available in the areas you have chosen. Think about where to find out more information – for example, books, journals, or trade papers. Study vacancies adverts in national and local newspapers.

Perhaps you could be helped by some sort of careers guidance. There are specific firms and organisations which give careers and vocational guidance. Some of these are specifically concerned with returning to work after a career-break. Others deal in counselling people after early retirement and redundancy. Most of these offer some sort of assessment and guidance. Don't ignore your local careers office and job club. Work out where you are going to find the time and the money and so on.

You will also need to check out any barriers that may be standing in your way, from practical ones such as not having anyone to look after your children (investigate childcare), to the internal barriers and doubts you may be placing in your own way. Check back to Chapter Seven for tips on dealing with these.

WHO CAN HELP

Think about the people who can help you – for example headhunters or professional jobfinders or consultants in your field. Think about what else you could do to learn more about the job you want, such as work experience, working part-time or as a volunteer. Learn to network. Find out whether there is a professional body, trade union, guild, or professional association linked to the field you want to enter – don't forget informal networks, people you know who work in the field you want to work in or who may know other people who might. Some organisations hold evening lectures or talks or lay on training courses, which may be of use. Don't forget your family and friends.

GOING SHOPPING

Shopping for a job is just like going shopping in any other market: before setting out, you need to consider whether there is a demand for your skills, whether the work is seasonal or subject to other constraints such as the weather, whether you have to be a particular age or gender, or have particular qualifications, whether you need any particular kind of experience?

DEVELOPING YOUR CAREER

If you are already in a job and you like the idea of going for a promotion, you need to think about whether this is possible within the company you are in or whether you will have to move. Consider whether the company is growing or static, the structure of the company and whether there are opportunities for upward movement. Think about the ambience of the company you work for – the working environment, style of management and so on – and whether it is something you feel happy with. Consider the usual length of time people spend in jobs in your company or field and the sort of money they can expect to earn – what is the most you could expect to earn and is it enough for you (refer back to Chapter Five)?

Then think about how best you could make your mark in your particular company or field. Do you need to move upwards, to increase your influence within a particular sphere i.e. move outwards? Would it help you to specialise in a particular area of knowledge, talents or skills and how easy or difficult is it to move from one area to another in your particular field?

IS SELF-EMPLOYMENT RIGHT FOR YOU?

There's never been a better time to set up and run your own business. The technology is there and large employers are finally cottoning on to how useful freelancers can be. Use the following checklist to see whether it might be right for you:

- I like the idea of being my own boss.
- I like the idea of being in control of my own working hours.
- I like the idea of using my own money to do something for me.
- I like the idea of being free.
- I like the idea of learning how to run a business.
- I like the idea of being able to work all the hours there are.
- I like the idea of being able to think up an idea for a business.
- I like the idea of being responsible for my own time and organisation.

How many did you tick? If you ticked all or most of them, then get started, using the five-step plan. Look back at the chapters on time and money management and think about how you would organise your working environment: would you work from home, rent an office, share space with other people doing something similar? If you choose to work at home, how will you separate home and work: should you have two telephones, a room you can close the door on, regular working hours? I know from my own experience how exciting working for yourself can be. But there are also times when it can be lonely and scary – I always think at the end of each month that no one is ever going to ask me to write an article again. Setting up support networks and getting the backing of your family are vital if you are to survive. But it's a step I have never regretted taking. To encourage you consider the following bonuses:

- Being self-employed means you will never be unemployed
- Being self-employed means increasing self-confidence
- Being self-employed means you can never be made redundant
- Being self-employed means you can control the amount of money you make
- Being self-employed means you will have plenty of experiences you can use later in life
- Being self-employed means you will be in control of your own life

Like the idea? Then go for it! Do remember that there are many different ways to get where you want to go. You don't always have to follow the conventional route. In some jobs experience may compensate for lack of formal qualifications.

CHECK YOUR PROGRESS

The fifth step in getting the work you want is to perform your final check. Set yourself a time limit and check your progress at set intervals to make sure you are still on course. You may, at the end of the day, find that you cannot get a job that meets all your needs and wants. In this case, you may decide that you could satisfy your skills, talents and interests in other ways, for example by what you do in your spare time. The list below gives a few ideas:

If you are a doer
- Cycling
- Horseriding
- Walking
- Windsurfing
- Scuba diving
- Football, cricket, hockey
- Cooking
- Making your own clothes

If you are a thinker
- Reading scientific or technical books and journals
- Observing, collecting, identifying wildlife, e.g. birds, animals, plants
- Going on geological or archeological expeditions
- Visiting museums
- Watching or listening to documentaries
- Playing chess
- Playing games such as Mastermind, Scrabble, Bridge
- Computer programming
- Tracing your family tree
- Meditation
- Attending lectures or evening classes in art history, science subjects, philosophy
  Add any other activities involving ideas that appeal to you

....

If you are a creator
- Learning an instrument or singing
- Writing a novel, short stories, poetry
- Drawing or painting
- Joining a drama group
- Doing a craft e.g. jewellery, pottery, weaving
- Going to art galleries, exhibitions, plays, concerts
- Photography
- Interior decorating

If you are a people person
- Organising parties or social events
- Doing things with friends e.g. going to the pub, restaurants, going out dancing, dinner parties
- Working with young children e.g. helping on the playgroup rota
- Sports, games and pastimes which involve other people such as sailing, joining a drama group, tennis
- Massage or aromatherapy
- Joining a personal growth group
- Travelling with friends or in a group
- Voluntary work

If you are an administrator
- Collecting coins, stamps, photos
- Keeping accounts
- Using computers, calculators for keeping records
- Acting as secretary, administrator or accountant to a voluntary, sports or social group
- Calligraphy

If you are an entrepreneur
- Backgammon, poker and other games of chance
- Following politics
- Being on a committee
- Selling things in your spare time
- Sports where winning is important such as motor racing, horse racing, tennis, squash and so on

GETTING THE WORK YOU WANT ROUND UP

Now you have read this chapter you should be well on the way to finding the job of your dreams. Tick the following:

- ☐ I can identify where my main skills, talents and interest lie.
- ☐ I can identify my transferrable skills.
- ☐ I know the area in which I want to work.
- ☐ I know whether I want to be self-employed.
- ☐ I will get the work I want.

CHAPTER NINE
GETTING THE RELATIONSHIP YOU WANT

Good relationships are important for all of us. Research shows that people who have an intimate relationship – it doesn't have to be with a sexual partner – are happier, more resilient and more able to cope with life. People who are married or in a permanent partnership even live longer. However it can be hard to find the partner of your dreams – and even harder to hold on to him or her. In this chapter, you will learn how to find the partner who is right for you, where to meet him or her, how to get closer once you have got together and when to stay or go if your relationship has run into difficulties. Bear in mind the five-step plan you have already read about in Part One and used to find the work that you want. Remember?

> Step one: Get in touch with your dream
>
> Step two: Research your dream
>
> Step three: Think out your plan of action
>
> Step four: Put your plan into action
>
> Step five: Check your progress

In fact, finding the partner you want has much in common with finding the job you want. You are simply not going to meet the man or woman of your dreams by sitting at home waiting for him or her to come ringing on your door bell. As with all other aspects of getting what you want you have to *do* something. And, just as when you are looking for a job, you work out what you want, do your research, and, if necessary, build up your skills. And just as you may have to apply for lots of jobs before you get accepted you may have to go out with many men or women – and experience a fair few rejections – before you find the one who is right for you. The myth of romantic love has a lot to answer for when it comes to getting what you want from a relationship. We've all been brought up to believe that Cupid's arrow strikes from the blue. In fact, most of us fall for people who are strikingly similar to us in attractiveness level, attitudes, age, religion, social class and various apects of personality. People are more likely to form long-term relationships if they are similar in height, share a similar interest in sport, have a similar way of looking at life. In fact, the only aspect of attraction where opposites attract is what psychologists describe as the witty–placid dimension. It seems that every comedian needs his or her fallguy! You may feel that it is thoroughly unromantic to go out looking for a partner with a 'shopping list'. But isn't it better – and fairer to the other person – to have worked out what you want from a relationship rather than embarking on one with no idea and then discovering that it wasn't what you wanted after all? In Part One you learnt to tap into your dreams, and now you are going to do that in your search for a partner.

YOUR PERFECT PARTNER

The degree of 'fit' between you and your partner's mental qualities, attitudes and personality is the foundation of a successful relationship. Physical aspects are also important when thinking about the sort of person you want to be with. Research shows that each of us has a 'lovemap' – a set of physical cues – that we have learnt to associate with sexual arousal. As you have discovered, many of us hark back to emotional patterns set in our childhood, and the physical cues that turn us on frequently have their origins in our past lives too. For example, if your much loved father had warm brown eyes and a crinkly smile, meeting a man who has these same attributes may make you melt. Alternatively, if your first girlfriend had blue eyes and a turned up nose, these physical traits may arouse you long after you have forgotten her name. Of course, 'lovemaps' can change: yours may be the classic tall, dark and handsome, but you may fall in love with someone who is short and fair, inevitably modifying your map. The exercise that follows will help you to build up your own blueprint of the partner you are looking for. But bear in mind that this isn't meant to be set in stone. Rather it is a mental checklist which you can use to help you in your search for a partner. The point is to decide how important each aspect of a potential partner is and how much it would matter if that particular aspect of him or her wasn't part of your relationship. Ideally it will help you get in touch with what you really want. In time you will develop a second sense that enables you to decide almost straightaway whether a particular person is right or wrong for you. You need some quiet time and a pen and notebook.

Now visualise your perfect partner in the way you discovered in Part One. Use the following checklist to specify the features and qualities you are looking for, and add any that you feel are especially important.

What I want in a partner	Essential	Slightly important	Unimportant
Looks			
Colour of eyes			
Colour of skin			
Colour of hair			
Height			
Build			
Anything else			

- **Mental qualities**

Practical

Intellectual

Creative

Organised

Enterprising

Sociable

Anything else

- **Achievements in**

The sciences

Sport

The creative world

Anything else

Personality

Extrovert

Sociable

Quiet

Reflective

Organised

Humorous

Anything else

Sexual orientation

Heterosexual

Bisexual

Gay

Now look through your list and pick out the most important attributes you want or need your partner to have.

The five most important attributes I want in my partner are:

- ....
- ....
- ....
- ....
- ....

You now have your blueprint for your perfect partner. Of course, the man or woman of your dreams may turn out to be quite the opposite of what you planned, but if you have some idea of what you are looking for and are aware of the most important attributes you will be in a much better position to spot Mr or Ms Right when they come along. If you choose someone who has what you want, and who in turn wants what you have, then you have the ingredients for a long and successful relationship.

THINKING ABOUT WHAT YOU WANT

If you've been on your own for a long time you may feel that you would be happy to settle for almost anyone, as long as you don't have to spend another night alone. However, a relationship that just satisfies a single need rarely stands the test of time. What often happens is that once that need has been satisfied, you change and other needs come to the fore — remember what we said about needs in Chapter One. Sadly, when this is the case, the relationship may founder. This is why relationships made when one or other partner is on the rebound often don't work out in the long run. Thinking about your needs and desires can help you to distinguish between those qualities which you consider essential and without which a relationship would never get off the ground, and those which you are willing to compromise.

Now you have a picture of your ideal partner, it's time to do a bit more research on what you are looking for in a relationship. It's important to be scrupulously honest with yourself about this and think about where you are now. Bear in mind that what you are looking for in a partner at 18 is unlikely to be the same as at 28, 38, 48, 58 or whatever. Are you looking for a long-term relationship, or are you seeking a short-term affair? How much time do you have in your life? Building a long-term relationship takes time. If you haven't got that time, and you are serious about finding a partner, you need to find some ways to create it (see Chapter Four) or shelve your search until a more suitable moment. Your knowledge of yourself that you have already gained by reading this far will help you here. If you are a 'people' person it may be important to have someone who wants to share your social life. If you are a thinker it may be more important to have someone with whom you can spend Saturday mornings discussing the meaning of life, the universe and everything. If you are a doer you may want someone who will help you build a boat or go out jogging with you. If you are an administrator, it may be important that your partner is very tidy too. If you are an entrepreneur you may want someone who can match you in energy and drive. Or, there again, none of these may apply; you may prefer someone who complements your qualities rather than matches them. Take your pen and notebook and write down answers to the following:

> **The nature of the commitment I want is:**
> - I want to spend time with my partner.
> - I want to live together/get married/other arrangement.
> - I want to share my bed/my house/my life.
> - Other things I want are..

> **The five most important things to me in a relationship are:**
> - I want someone I can talk to about ideas.
> - I want someone who will share my social life.
> - I want someone who observes my need for 'me' time.
> - I want someone who accepts my children.
> - Other things I want are: ....

LEARNING ABOUT RELATIONSHIPS

As you know by now, any plan of action must start from where you are now. And part of where you are now is, of course, where you have been. This applies as much to relationships as to any other area of your life. To consider an extreme example: if you were emotionally or physically abused as a child, you may find it hard to trust yourself and others or find yourself getting into similar abusive relationships as an adult.

To find out what you are bringing to a relationship use a page in your notebook and examine your relationship history. List the most significant relationships you have had so far in your life. Include your parents, your sisters and brothers, grandparents, former boyfriends or girlfriends and take time to reflect on what messages you acquired about yourself and relationships. For example, the woman who learnt from her mother that there are two types of men – the wild, dashing type you fall in love with and the sensible type that you marry – may in adult life marry someone she finds reliable but dull and end up having constant affairs.

> Important people in my life so far:
>
> | Who | What it taught me about relationships |
> |-----|---------------------------------------|
> | .... | .... |
> | .... | .... |

What did you discover? From now on try to be aware of any unhelpful beliefs that you are bringing to your relationships. Try to keep an open mind about the person you meet. Remember this is a unique individual, with his or her good points and faults, just like you, and try not to let people in your past get in the way.

FORMING A RELATIONSHIP

The next stage of your campaign is to use what you have learned by doing the above exercises to help you set goals about what you are looking for in a relationship. Don't forget to make them specific, positive and active. Once you have done this you are ready to start looking.

MEETING THE PARTNER OF YOUR DREAMS

You may think you have to make special plans in order to meet your dreamboat. In fact, all you have to do is use the opportunities in your everyday life. Opportunities to meet a partner are all around you – once you have decided to look. Research into where people meet their partners suggests that most people meet at work or in work-linked activities or while socialising. Mutual friends have been a favourite way of meeting members of the opposite sex for time immemorial. The main thing is to cast your net as wide as possible to enable you to meet as many potential partners as you can. Think about where you have met partners in the past, how much time you can afford to spend looking, and any other considerations that might make a difference to your goals or time scale, such as the ticking of your biological clock. If there are, be sure to make allowances for them in your plans. If you are pushing 39 and determined to have a baby, you need to be more proactive than if you are 19. Here are some ideas for where to meet:

- Friends and relatives
- Adult education classes
- Voluntary activities
- Health clubs and gyms

- Out and about: the supermarket, launderette, railway station, cafes and restaurants
- Dance classes
- Nightclubs
- Wine bars and pubs
- Rambling and youth hostelling
- Parties
- Work and work-linked activities
- Public events: concerts, plays
- Bookshops and libraries
- Contact clubs, dating agencies and marriage bureaux
- Lonely hearts ads

Don't dismiss these last as 'artificial', they can work very well, especially for people who know what they want. Louise is a case in point.

- *Divorced and working full-time with two small children to look after, she had very little spare time. However she did want to meet another partner. She reckoned that she only had one evening a week to devote to this, so she decided to spend some money on joining a dating agency. After thinking carefully about the sort of man she wanted to meet she spent some more time looking at the different agencies. She settled on one that had a high proportion of men and women who work in the media and creative world, which is where she herself worked. Six months later she met Ron, a theatre director with whom she now lives. Louise could have left it all to chance. Instead she planned an effective way to ensure that she met suitable partners who met her specifications.*

Once you have your list of places where you might meet a partner make sure you incorporate them into goals: for example plan to start an evening class on a particular day, and then do it. Of course, it's not enough just to go to these places. You have to talk to people if you are to meet them, so look back at Chapter Six and brush up on your conversational skills.

IS THIS WHO YOU WANT?

Let's imagine you have met the man or woman of your dreams. How do you make sure that the person who has what you want wants you? In the first flush of romance it's easy to assume that your partner has the same aims in mind – but you could be wrong. Far too many relationships founder because people assume that their partner is in it for the same reasons as they are, without bothering to check. A classic mismatch happens when one partner's motives are purely sexual, while the other is looking for long-term commitment. Nothing wrong with good old-fashioned lust of course, so long as you are both clear where you stand and are happy to enjoy the relationship for what it is. But if you persist in the hope that the other person is going to change his or her mind, then you could end up being extremely miserable. Change is possible, of course, but your partner must have the desire to change. And though it's a fact that where there's a will there's a way, it's equally true to say where there is no will there is no way. You may be better off cutting your losses and finding someone who is a better match for your needs.

On the other hand you can't expect every relationship to give you everything you want. If your partner doesn't fulfil your needs you have two options: either to discontinue the relationship or to try to find the things which are missing in other ways, from friends, relatives, and workmates, and from other activities. The option you choose will depend on how many of your needs your partner is meeting, and where these needs stand in your overall list of priorities.

Look at the checklist and tick the ones that apply to you. Now be brave (and honest) and tick the ones that apply to your partner:

- Lust
- Companionship
- Loneliness
- All my friends have someone

- Someone to show off
- Someone to confide in
- Someone to ease the pain of a relationship break-up
- Someone to make me feel good about myself
- Someone to love
- Someone to love me
- Long-term commitment

If your reasons for being together match, then your partnership stands every chance of developing. If they don't, you need to decide whether it has enough of what you want to make it worthwhile. Don't assume your partner will change: s/he may – or may not.

CEMENTING THE BOND

So, once you have found a partner how do you foster feelings of closeness? There is evidence that the greater the range of activities couples share, the more likely their relationship is to stand the test of time. On the other hand, wanting to do fewer things together can be a sign that the other person is drawing away from the relationship. At the courtship stage doing things together also enables you to observe your partner in different situations and see how compatible you are. After all, if his idea of a lazy Sunday afternoon is to sit in front of the TV with a can of lager watching the football and yours is sitting sipping kir on the patio, you are both going to need to learn to compromise. Later on, of course, the things you do together are likely to change in nature from the things we've mentioned to things like having a baby together, buying a house, and so on.

How does your relationship shape up?

Tick the activities you have done with your partner in the past week:

1. Having fun together
- Went to a party
- Went dancing
- Went to the theatre
- Saw a film
- Visited friends
- Went out for a meal
- Add any others you and your partner did ....

2. Spending your spare time in joint leisure activities
- Did something outdoors, e.g. sailing, windsurfing, tennis, cycling, walking
- Did something indoors, e.g. visited a museum, art exhibition, lecture
- Attended an evening class together
- Went to a sporting event, e.g. football match, tennis match
- Add any others you and your partner did ....

3. Intimacy
- Discussed a personal problem
- Talked about your beliefs and feelings
- Gave one another a massage
- Made love
- Add any others you and your partner did ....

4. Practicalities
- Did the housework

- Went to the launderette
- Prepared a meal
- Went to the supermarket
- Add any others you and your partner did ....

Now think about ways you can get closer by doing even more things together.

You read in Part One about how important good communication is in getting what you want, and love relationships are no exception. Learning how to talk to and listen to each other are the keys to getting and staying close. Psychologists have discovered that in good relationships partners talk to each other more, confide in each other more, are more likely to face up to problems in a constructive way, show more love, approval, affection, encouragement and respect (both verbally and non-verbally), make more positive statements about the behaviour of the other person and are more sensitive to each other's feelings. Happy couples laugh more together and indulge in their own private language and jokes – if you think of the Valentine messages from 'Furry Bunny to Big Bear' that appear in the national newspapers every year you'll appreciate the sort of thing I mean! Unhappy relationships on the other hand tend to be characterised by disagreeing more and belittling each other through criticism, blame or sarcasm, and are also less affectionate physically. If things go wrong, they are more likely to let problems fester and less likely to face up to them try and to put things right. They tend to argue more and hold grudges for longer.

OVERCOMING THE BARRIERS

You saw in Part One how having a losing mentality can affect the way you perceive experiences and events and the way you behave. Well, the same applies to relationships.

> How many of these beliefs do you hold? Tick the statements that apply to you:
>
> - Arguing is destructive to relationships.
> - I believe that if my partner really loved me s/he would know what I need without me having to tell him/her.
> - I believe that a leopard can't change it's spots.
> - I believe that I have to be the perfect lover.
> - I believe that men and women are different.

These are classic examples of dangerous beliefs that can make you disappointed and disillusioned with your relationship. Focusing on these beliefs and transforming them into positive thoughts in the way you have already learnt in Chapter Seven helps to prevent you from growing apart.

BEAT YOUR LOSING BELIEFS

- Be prepared to tackle your differences. Some conflict in a relationship is only natural. It's not arguing that is destructive but failing to tackle disagreements in a constructive way.
- Be honest about your desires and feelings. No matter how much your partner loves you s/he can't read your mind. It's up to you to tell him/her what your needs and wants are.
- Change is possible if the motivation is there. People can and do change – otherwise why are you reading this book? Being open with each other about your feelings is the first step towards change.
- There is no such thing as the perfect lover. In bed, as out of bed, there is no such thing as perfection. Different people have different needs and wants. Honest communication is the key to ensuring that you satisfy each other.
- Your partner is a unique individual with unique desires and

needs. Men and women sometimes approach things from different perspectives because of the way in which they are brought up and the things they feel are expected of them. However, being open and honest with each other will help you understand your partner as a human being and not just a representative of his/her sex.

WHAT'S STOPPING YOU?

Sometimes, no matter how much you think you want a loving relationship every partnership you embark upon seems to end in disaster. In this case there may be deeper underlying reasons why you are finding it difficult to relate closely to a partner. By bringing your fears out into the open and tackling them they can be sorted out. Do any of the following ring a bell?

- 'I am afraid of being hurt or rejected'. If you have experienced a lot of pain in your past relationships you may be so afraid of being hurt again that you hold back in this relationship. Ironically enough, this can create exactly the situation you most fear – a self-fulfilling prophecy.
- 'I am afraid of being swamped/losing my identity'. Women in particular often seem to lose their identity in relationships. Psychologists say this is because as children girls identify with their mothers so never have to separate from them in the way little boys do.
- 'I'm afraid that once my partner sees my faults s/he won't love me any more'. The roots of this fear often lie in perfectionism, which as we saw in Part One can be so destructive.
- 'I'm afraid I my feelings are so strong that I will destroy the relationship'. If you feel like this, chances are you have been taught that feelings are bad.
- 'I'm afraid that if I open up to my partner s/he will use what I reveal against me'. It could be that you are with a manipulative partner, who will indeed do what you fear. In which case the answer may be to get out. On the other hand it could be your own fears that are stopping you. You won't know until you try.

- 'I am afraid of losing control'. Again you won't know until you trust your partner enough to show your true self. In healthy partnerships, no one person is in control; the balance of power is even.

DEALING WITH DISAGREEMENTS

However much you love each other you are bound to disagree from time to time. The following problem-solving technique can help you to deal with your disagreements so they don't turn into major rows.

- Define the real problem. Very often what appears to be the problem on the surface isn't the real issue. For example the problem 'Shall we spend this Christmas with your parents or my parents?' could be more to do with the fact that you feel resentful because you never seem to spend time alone with your partner. In this case you may need to define the problem differently, 'How to find a way to spend some time alone together this Christmas.' You need to dig down and ask questions so that you can discover the true source of the problem. Give yourself time to think to sift through the facts and separate facts from opinions.
- Once you have defined what the problem is, it's time to think about possible solutions. At this stage it may help to write down all the possible solutions no matter how hare-brained or impossible they appear at first sight. For example, some solutions to finding time to spend together over Christmas; 'To spend Christmas alone and organise a party at New Year with both sets of parents'; 'To ask one set of parents on Christmas Eve, the other on Christmas Day and to spend Boxing Day alone'; 'To agree that Christmas is too busy a time to spend alone, but to promise yourselves to spend some time alone together before or after and book some holiday so you can do so'; 'To take off to a tropical island for a diving holiday together and escape Christmas altogether.'
- Put first things first. How important is this problem? If it's not important it doesn't matter what you decide. To help you decide

on the importance of the problem, ask yourself: what difference will it make one year from now?
- Analyse. What are the implications of the various solutions you have brainstormed? Can you put some of the solutions together. How could you reach a compromise? Will it hurt anyone? Include yourself in this. Don't be confused between real hurt and 'necessary pain'.
- Act. Order the jumbo-sized turkey. Ring up your parents and tell them that you won't be seeing them for Christmas this year. Book that holiday in the Maldives . . .

MAKING THE RELATIONSHIP YOU HAVE BETTER

Doing an occasional emotional health check is important in any relationship if you are to stay close and avoid small problems stacking up and becoming larger ones. Here are a few tips:

- Don't let things drift. Few of us like conflict and it's all too easy to let things carry on the way they are for fear of upsetting your partner or because you are afraid of being alone. This is extremely damaging to both your and your partner's self-esteem. There's no need to have heavy discussions every night of the week, but tackling your differences as and when they occur helps ensure that tiny problems don't build up.
- Beware of hidden messages. It's all too easy when talking to your partner to avoid the real issue by not saying what you really mean. For example, 'What you really mean to say is that you feel lonely left on your own'. Your partner needs to know how you feel – s/he may think that you are perfectly happy with his/her behaviour.
- Pick your moment carefully. If you are going to have a difficult discussion with your partner don't pick a moment when s/he is rushed, tired after a day at work or irritable. Research also shows that if your partner has done something to annoy you, not lashing out straightaway, as you may feel inclined to do, enables

more constructive communication to take place too. So next time your partner says something that makes you see red, allow yourself a few seconds before responding. Go and put the kettle on, switch off the TV – anything to give yourself a bit of breathing space.

- Use open-ended questions. Closed questions only allow your partner to answer one thing. For example to the question, 'Are you feeling miserable?' your partner can only answer 'Yes' or 'No'. Open-ended questions on the other hand, such as 'I sense that you are feeling miserable, what is on your mind?' enable you to explore more fully exactly what is bothering the other person.

- Use 'I' language. Your partner is more likely to listen to what you have to say if you avoid criticism and blame. And it is much less threatening if you tell him or her how his or her behaviour affects you rather than launching a swingeing attack on his or her character. For example, 'You forgot to buy me flowers again on Valentine's Day, it proves you don't love me, you made me feel so angry,' is blaming and immediately puts your partner on the defensive. After all *you* are responsible for your own feelings. A more constructive way of putting things is to say, 'When you forgot it was Valentine's Day and didn't buy me any flowers I felt angry.' Try to focus on the specifics of a situation too, rather than making global assertions such as, 'Whenever we go out, you're always looking at other women.'

- Pay attention to body language. 85% of our communication is non-verbal. Learn to tune into your partner's body language – posture, facial expression, habits such as chewing his or her lip, frowning, curling his or her hair, the tone of voice s/he uses when s/he is excited or angry, the speed at which s/he speaks when s/he is upset about something. All these can tell you an enormous amount about the way your partner is feeling and increase the sense of understanding and being understood.

- Check that you understand what your partner is saying or feeling. Many misunderstandings occur because we don't really listen to what our partner is saying and assume that we know. At various points in the conversation, saying something like, 'So you're saying that . . .' or, 'You felt really jealous/angry/depressed when . . .' makes sure that you stay on the same wavelength and helps your partner to feel understood.

WHEN THINGS GO WRONG

However much you want it, not every relationship can end with you both walking off into the sunset together. Although parting is sad, it's far better to leave a partner who isn't what you really want, than to spend the rest of your life in a relationship that isn't really right for you. Painful though it is, you can eventually use the knowledge you have gained about yourself and your needs to look for a relationship that is more what you want. However, deciding to go or stay is not always that easy. Sometimes the issue is clear cut: a partner who abuses you, undermines you or belittles you physically is not worth staying for – ever. But often there aren't any clear solutions. In this case, it may help to use the problem-solving technique described above. Sometimes putting a bit of space between you and your partner by having a trial separation helps. At other times, decision-making is a long, hard process that one or both of you reach reluctantly. Using the tactics you have learned in *How To Get What You Want* can help you decide whether this relationship is the one you want or whether it is better to leave and try to find one that is better for you.

By and large the following are *not* sufficient on their own to stay in a partnership that has gone badly wrong:

- I've invested a lot of time and effort in it and I don't want to let it go.
- My Mum and Dad want me to get married.
- I/my partner wants a baby.
- Everyone else I know is married.
- I might not find anyone better.
- No one else will ever love me.

PREPARING YOURSELF FOR PARTING

Just as you need to marshall your resources when entering a relationship, so you need to do your research when you plan to go. You need to know that you will be able to cope alone. Using visualisation can help you imagine what lies ahead and prepare you to cope with it, so that you have the strength to go through with your decision. What will you miss? What will you be glad to have got rid of? How will your life change? Think about whether you will continue to see your partner, and if so what will this involve. If you have children you will usually have to negotiate some way in which they can see both their parents. Some couples find having a complete break from each other for a time allows them to redefine their relationship on different terms. Recognise that breaking up is hard to do (it scores as one of the top ten most stressful life events) and be kind to yourself. See Chapter Thirteen for more tips on this.

- Face up to your fear of being unhappy. Yes, you may well feel miserable for a while, and if you don't you may well question what the relationship had going for it. Allow yourself to experience your feelings of sadness. How will you express your sadness – think back to other occasions in the past when you had to deal with unhappiness. Will you cry, get angry, sink into gloomy introspection, play sad records, write in your diary, paint the house? Now remind yourself that you will be able to cope with the feelings of sadness. Give yourself time to express your emotions, but don't allow them to overwhelm you. Think about what or who helped you in the past. Was it talking to friends, visiting a therapist, giving yourself bodily treats like a massage, making yourself a special meal that you particularly enjoyed? Could they help again? Make a list of things you can do: book an evening class, book a holiday, arrange to see a friend, take up a sport or hobby that s/he would have hated, get yourself some paid work.
- Enjoy your freedom. Many people stay in relationships that are wrong for them because they fear being alone. In fact there is nothing more lonely than being with someone you don't want

to be with. Instead, learn to revel in your solitude. Think what a gift time to yourself will be: how wonderful to start the day as *you* want. To linger over breakfast in bed, with all the food that you like, to dress in the clothes you want to wear, to spend some time pottering in the garden, to listen to the music that you want to listen to without a partner to drag you down.

- Enlist the help of others. Think of all the people who could help support you. List those who you could call for a quick chat over the phone. Next list those who you think would be able and willing to spend some time with you going to the cinema, theatre or a meal.
- Use the time you save to pursue one of your aims. If you have a full life then missing out on one part of it – a relationship – is less devastating than if you have built your entire existence around your partner. Women in particular are often guilty of letting their lives revolve around their man. Not surprisingly, if the relationship fails their life seems empty. Now is the time to realise some of your other wants or goals. Have a look at the other sections of this book: is there something you want to change about your appearance or self-image, perhaps, is there a job or career you have always dreamed of pursuing, a trip you have always longed to take?

GETTING THE RELATIONSHIP YOU WANT ROUND UP

Now you have read to the end of this chapter you are well on the way to getting the healthy, happy relationships you deserve. So now read the following list and check on what you have learnt:

> ☐ I am prepared to work at finding the relationship that is right for me.
>
> ☐ I am prepared to make an effort to understand the way I and my partner relate to each other.

- [ ] I am committed to developing the knowledge and skills to enable me to improve and develop my relationships.

- [ ] I am willing to acknowledge when there are problems in the relationship.

- [ ] I am prepared to look honestly at my own behaviour and see what part it is playing in any problems.

- [ ] I am willing to seek outside help if my partner and I find it impossible to sort out problems together.

- [ ] I am prepared to leave the relationship if it is not possible to make the necessary changes.

If you've ticked all seven boxes, you are now ready for the next chapter in which you will find out how to look the way you want.

CHAPTER TEN
LOOKING THE WAY YOU WANT

You may not have given a lot of thought to the way you look until now. But the fact is that if you look good, you feel good. And feeling good is a big boost to confidence and self-worth, which in turn is vital to getting what you want. Of course, confidence is more than skin deep; you have to believe in yourself as well. However, looking as good as you can and feeling happy with the way you look can help give you that inner radiance that helps you to get what you want in other areas of your life.

In this chapter you will learn about how to give yourself a new image and how to feel good about yourself and project yourself in a way that truly reflects you. You will learn how you can change your shape through diet, exercise, or even cosmetic surgery and how you can wear the clothes that flatter you and reflect you as you are. Bear in mind the five-step plan outlined in Part One. You must remember it by now:

> Step one: Get in touch with your dream
>
> Step two: Research your dream
>
> Step three: Think out your plan of action
>
> Step four: Put your plan into action
>
> Step five: Check your progress

GETTING IN TOUCH WITH YOUR DREAM

Just for a moment, imagine yourself as you would like to be if you were to look exactly the way you wanted. Let your imagination run as wild and free as you like: Madonna's figure, Cindy Crawford's face, Mel Gibson's eyes? You can have them all – in your dreams. Now analyse your dream and think about what it tells you about the way you feel about the way you look. There's often a lot of pressure on us to be perfect. It certainly isn't the aim of this chapter to encourage you to feel discontented with yourself the way you are, but there may well be elements of your dream that you can tap into to make decisions about how you can be the best possible *you*. For instance, if you want a figure like Madonna's, yet when you look in the mirror all you see is a sagging belly and cellulite pitted thighs, you need to think about how to tone up. Even if you don't achieve a Madonna hourglass you will certainly feel better about yourself.

MIRROR, MIRROR ON THE WALL

As with any changes you want to make, if you want to change the way you look you need to start from where you are.

> Using a page in your notebook, stand in front of a mirror and describe what you see – honestly. Start with your facial features like chin, nose, eyes, eyebrows, hair type and hair colour, ears and mouth, then look at your body and describe its bone structure, build, fat composition, skin, skin colour, skin type, legs, arms, body hair, feet, hands – in fact, everything you can think of about your appearance. Do not be tempted to judge your appearance – simply describe.
>
> Now you have analysed what you look like, note down ten things you like and ten things you dislike about your appearance:
>
> - Ten things I like about my appearance are ....
> - Ten things I dislike about my appearance are ....

> Everyone has some good points, so don't be modest, write them down and congratulate yourself for your soft hair, long eyelashes and so on.

Now look at your dislikes list and think about what you want to do about them. It could be that you are actually quite happy with the way you are. If so, fine. There's no need to read any further. OK so your belly is a bit bigger than you would ideally like it to be, but you can always wear baggy sweaters and you have shapely breasts, or your chin isn't exactly Kevin Costner's but you can always grow a beard. Remember the 'cost-benefit' analysis you learnt how to do when thinking about making changes in Chapter Two. You can apply it to your appearance too and decide whether you feel it is worth making any changes. If you do decide to change, then read on – you'll find several suggestions.

HOW MUCH YOU CAN CHANGE?

Up to a point, of course, the way you look is determined by your genes and your basic bone structure. Like Michael Jackson, there's no way you can turn a black skin white or vice versa without spending a great deal of time and money. Similarly it's hard if not impossible to turn curly hair straight, brown eyes blue – though you could always try coloured contact lenses – or make you a 5 foot 11 inch blonde supermodel if you are a curvaceous 4 foot 10 inch brunette.

If you do find yourself wanting something completely impossible, think about what your fantasy is telling you. Why do you want to be a supermodel – fame, money, admiration? And why do you want those things? Is it because deep down you feel you aren't acceptable as you are? If so, working on your self-esteem to help you feel better about yourself could do far more than submitting yourself to the surgeon's knife.

Once you have decided what you want to change use the brainstorming technique you have already learnt to think about all the ways you could bring about changes and analyse them to see what you would have to do to put them into action. Once you have some ideas you are ready to set some goals and targets for yourself.

CHANGING THE WAY YOU LOOK

SOME EASY WAYS TO CHANGE YOUR APPEARANCE

Remember the distinction between short-term and long-term goals? Well, you can create some short-term goals to change the way you look now. How about the following:

- Change your clothes
- Buy a new hair colour
- Experiment with a new way of doing your make-up (women)
- Make an appointment to have your hair cut
- Buy a new outfit or alter an old one

Long-term goals are things that are going to involve you in a longer committment:

- Lose five stone in weight
- Reshape your body through exercise
- Grow a beard
- Let yourself go grey

Once you have set your goals, remember to check that they are active, specific and positive and if necessary break them down into smaller targets and think about how you are going to achieve them. For example, if you are planning to lose five stone in weight, how will you do it? Join a slimming club? Go it alone? Buy a book or video? Have your stomach clamped? If you are planning extensive orthodontistry or cosmetic surgery you will need to find the funds, organise time off work, work out who is the best person to do it, get the support of your friends and family and so on.

WORKING WITH WHAT YOU'VE GOT

Make-up artist Barbara Daly, who created the Body Shop range of cosmetics, says,

The first stage is accepting what you really look like . . . concentrate

> *on how you perceive yourself, not what other people think of you . . . adapt the look to suit yourself.*

'Hear! Hear! As with everything else, changing your image works best if you start from the raw material you already have.

In terms of our body build most of us fall into one of three basic types (see box below). Appearances can be deceptive, however, because few of us are purely one or another, and however slim you are you can still put on weight. If an ectomorph, or lean, thin person puts on fat, they may still look slim, and weigh less (fat weighs less than muscle) while still having quite a high proportion of fat to muscle. Equally, you can be a mesomorph, muscular type, and also be quite hefty.

Mesomorph: Muscular body with a high proportion of large, fast muscle fibres

Best exercise: Jumping, throwing, sprinting

Ectomorph: Slim, lean build, with high proportion of small, slow muscle fibres

Best exercise: Long-term aerobic endurance such as marathons, walking

Endomorph: Soft, rounded appearance with a tendency to lay down fat. Harder to develop good muscle definition

Best exercise: Swimming, weights and exercise systems

DO YOU NEED TO LOSE WEIGHT?

Body fat in itself is not necessarily a sign that you are unhealthy so you shouldn't feel pressurised into being slim. Women carry twice the fat of men yet on average live four or five years longer. In the past few years, scientists have discovered that weight in isolation is actually a fairly crude measure of whether or not you are dangerously overweight. A more accurate method of finding out whether you need to lose some weight is to calculate what the experts call your body mass index (BMI) or the amount of fat you are carrying in relation to your height. To do this you will need:

- A pen.
- A ruler or tape measure in metres.
- A calculator.
- A notebook.

To find your BMI measure your height in metres. Now square this figure by multiplying it by itself. Weigh yourself in kilograms and divide your weight by the square of your height. Now check the following list:

If you are a man:

20 or less	Underweight
20.1–25	Acceptable
25.1–29.9	Overweight
30+	Very overweight

If you are a woman:

18.6 or less	Underweight
18.7–23.8	Acceptable
23.9–28.5	Overweight
28.6 or more	Very overweight

If your BMI is 28.6 or over if you are a woman, or 30 or over if you are a man, then you certainly need to lose weight, for the sake of your health as well as your appearance. On the other hand, if your BMI is between 23.9 and 28.5 if you are a woman and 25.1 and 29.9 if you are a man, the picture is a bit fuzzier.

CHANGING YOUR BODY WITH DIET

Changing your diet and exercising are two very effective ways to change your body shape. The emphasis these days is not so much on rigid self-denial so much as eating healthily. Remember that food is for enjoying and that this does not mean banning all the things you like. Even if you are overweight you can allow yourself the odd chocolate bar, just so long as you don't go overboard. The best way to switch to a healthy eating plan is to make small changes in the way you eat by setting yourself small, achievable goals in the way you have now learnt. Changing your diet dramatically overnight is unlikely to last. Remember: you don't have to stop eating any foods, just eat less of some and more of others. It's beyond the scope of this book to go into much detail on what you should aim to eat. But if you need some ideas there are any number of books on the market. Check your diet by looking at the following checklist.

> Aim to eat:
>
> - Four or five portions of bread, cereals and potatoes a day
> - Five portions of fruit and vegetables (around 1lb) a day
> - Two portions of meat, fish or vegetable proteins such as pulses, nuts and so on a day
> - Two portions of milk, cheese or yoghurt a day
> - Very occasional treats of biscuits, cakes, sweets, chocolate, jam, crisps

A word about fats: butter, margarine, spreads, cooking fats and oils are high in calories and harder to burn off through exercise, so keep them to the minimum. The latest thinking is that we should all eat less saturated fats (hard or animal fats), and more monounsaturated fats and oils such as olive oils and omega-3 fatty acids found in fish oils.

If the way you eat reflects the above eating plan, then congratulations. If not, use the information to make an eating plan and set yourself some targets. Don't forget to check occasionally to make sure you are still on course.

CHANGING YOUR BODY WITH EXERCISE

Regular exercise can help you to burn up fat and lose weight, though the type of exercise needed in each case tends to be slightly different. For fitness, the intensity of your exercise, in other words how hard you exercise, is the most important factor. For weight loss, the main factor is the number of calories you use. For better definition of your muscles you need to work your muscles often – so working with weights and exercise systems such as Pilates are best. You'll find plenty of ideas for the kind of exercises and activities you might choose in the next chapter, but if you are having difficulty sticking to an exercise plan, check out some of the following motivators:

> - By starting to exercise, my body will develop more muscle, which will boost my body's metabolic rate and help me stabilise my weight
>
> - Regular exercise will help my appetite control
>
> - Regular exercise will help me to feel better mentally
>
> - Regular exercise will give me more energy

Convinced? Then get down to setting yourself some goals. Remember to make them very specific – not just 'take more exercise' but 'go to a step class three times a week starting on July 20th' or whatever. Make sure you keep a record of your progress to keep up your motivation.

CHANGING YOUR BODY WITH CLOTHES

As a self-confessed clothes addict, the Victorian philosopher Thomas Carlisle's adage, 'Beware any enterprise that requires new clothes,' never made a lot of sense to me. Your clothes say a lot about you, so make sure they really reflect the person you want to be, not the person you think you ought to be, or your mother thought you ought to be 30 years ago. Think about what your clothes say about you. Experiment with different looks and colour. If you have always opted for sensible classics, but secretly longed to be glamorous or rock star chic, go a little wild occasionally. Sticking to the safest option is just as much a bad habit as running up your credit card bill every time you go walking down the high street. Check that your clothes match your lifestyle. Make your clothes work for you by being aware of your roles and the image you project.

Learn to play up your best features and play down your worst. If you have a curvaceous figure, avoid anything too tight or with too many gathers; if you have a tendency to be top-heavy go for vertical stripes and open neck collars on top, horizontal lines to add width at hip level. But don't become obsessed – if you like something and feel confident wearing it, then forget all the rules. Above all, wear your clothes – don't let them wear you.

CHANGING YOUR BODY WITH COSMETIC SURGERY

Cosmetic surgery is the most drastic way of changing your appearance. Not only does it cost money but it is irreversible. Cosmetic surgery is getting more popular and more accessible for ordinary people. But before you embark on it, bear in mind why you are doing it and check your expectations. Be aware of who is pulling your strings. Do it for you, not to get back at people in your past or to erase negative messages. Cindy Jackson, who has spent more than £30,000 and six years on turning herself into a living Barbie doll, said in an interview in the *Daily Mail*, 'Both my mother and sister were pretty, but I never was. All through my childhood people constantly told me, "Oh you look just like your Dad." And I'd look in the mirror and see his stupid face. I hated him. I hated him with every fibre of my being.' No prizes for guessing who is pulling her strings.

The fact is changing the shape of your nose or having the fat sucked from your thighs isn't going to bring you the relationship or the job you want, although once you've had your nose job or liposuction you may have the confidence to go out and get the things you want. No-one split up with their husband or wife just because their nose was the wrong shape or because they had crow's feet around the eyes. And if your partner only loves you for what you look like, you almost certainly need to think long and hard about what such a relationship is worth, and whether it is worth saving. On the other hand, relationships can split up because one person's self-consciousness about their big nose, droopy breasts or baggy eyelids is causing them to become miserable and reclusive. Think carefully about what cosmetic surgery can and can't do for you. Many reputable plastic surgeons today employ counsellors to help people considering surgery to examine their motives and expectations.

If you do decide to go ahead, think about what you want, consider costs and timing (will you need time off work? how much surgery do you want? over what period of time?) and so on. Be realistic about exactly what you can hope to achieve — a reputable surgeon should be able to give you a good idea.

IT'S YOUR CHOICE

As we have seen, there are hundreds of ways to look more the way you want. Just to prove it to you have a look at the following ways of changing your appearance and think about whether you would like to try any of them. Remember, it's your body — and your choice.

BREASTS

- Exercise. Swimming is particularly good for shaping the bust, and you could also try working with fixed or free weights at the gym, or some of the special bust-tightening exercises you can find in exercise books and videos.
- Your bra. Try a smooth well-fitting bra if your breasts are on the heavy side, and wear a special sports bra for exercising to prevent discomfort. If you want to add a bit of oomph to your bust try a padded or uplift bra.
- Big and particularly sudden increases or decreases in weight can cause the breasts to sag and lose tone, so try to keep your weight fairly constant.

- Cosmetic surgery. Breast enlargement operations are some of the most popular. The jury is still out on whether the silicon used in breast implants is harmful. (It's used very successfully for making chins and cheeks bigger and increasing the height of the nose.) Surgeon Dev Basra, who has been responsible for more than a few celebrity nips and tucks, says, 'Silicon is a really great fat substitute. It is a synthetic substance which has always been considered safe. It is its misuse that makes it unsafe.' Surgeons are using newer materials nowadays. However, Dev Basra admits, 'There isn't a perfect implant.' It's still possible to breastfeed if you have a breast implant, unless too much tissue has been removed.

FACE

- Watch your beauty routine. Use one of the anti-ageing moisturisers that contain AHAs (alpha hydroxy acids), fruit acids which give a mild chemical peel, erasing fine lines and keeping your skin smooth and clear. Most beauty preparations contain these.
- Exercise and massage. You can't change your underlying bone structure; however, you can try some of the face exercises designed to strengthen and tone up the underlying muscles of the face, resulting in fewer lines and wrinkles. Regular aromatherapy massage is another good way to improve circulation to the face, giving younger looking skin and enhanced muscle tone.
- Electrical techniques (face lift without surgery). There are various forms of this treatment which use a mild electric current to tone the underlying muscles of the face for a fraction of the cost you would pay for a surgical face lift. The therapist usually does one side of your face first on the initial treatment so you can see the degree of lift. The result is usually a subtle, but definite uplift which makes you look brighter, more alert and younger. A course of around six intensive treatments is recommended followed by regular top-ups. Available at beauty salons.

- Chemical peeling. This treatment, which must be done by a specialist dermatologist (skin doctor), involves using a mild caustic preparation to burn off the outer layers of skin. It can be used to remove fine surface lines and improve skin texture. Available from specialist cosmetic surgery clinics.
- Dermabrasion. The surface layer of the skin is abraded with brushes and discs using a special machine a bit like a mini 'Black and Decker' sanding machine, so removing fine lines and scarring. Available from specialist cosmetic surgery clinics.
- Hibernation treatment. A bacteria called botulin is injected just above the muscles blocking messages from the brain to the muscle and knocking out habits like frowning which cause lines and wrinkling. Useful for frown lines, brow lines, laughter lines and lines around the eyes and on the chin to stop excessive dimpling.
- Collagen implants. Collagen, a gluey protein made by the skin which plumps out the cells and is lost as we age, is injected into fine lines and wrinkles or the lips to produce a 'bee stung' look. Available from specialist cosmetic surgery clinics.
- Face lift (rhytidectomy). By far the most drastic solution, a full face lift used to involve a three-hour operation in which the skin on the neck and face is lifted and re-shaped and excess skin trimmed away. Today surgeons are beginning to use keyhole techniques so the lift can be peformed without a major cut. However some surgeons believe unless you lift a lot of skin you are not going to be able to get rid of sagging jowls and chin and crepey, ageing neck. Mini-lifts can also be done – a bit like tightening a screw – but are said to be better for people who have already had a lift or those who are medically unfit for a full face lift.
- Lid lift (blepharoplasty). Used to correct puffy or crepey upper eyelids and bags beneath the lower eyelids. An incision is made in the socket of the upper eyelid and just below the lashes of the lower lid, allowing excess skin or fatty tissue to be removed.
- Nose job (rhinoplasty). One of the most successful cosmetic surgery operations. The skin is lifted off the cartilage and bone

allowing the surgeon to remodel them; the skin is then reshaped and stretched back over the nose. All stitching is done from inside the nostrils so there are no visible scars.

THIGHS

- Exercise. Cycling, swimming and exercising on machines against resistance are all good.
- Massage can help break down cellulite.
- Liposuction, in which fat is sucked from the thighs. Today ultrasonic liposuction which breaks the fat down first is being used very successfully.

ABDOMEN

- Exercises such as sit-ups, the crunch and swimming can help.
- Liposuction again.

LOOKING THE WAY YOU WANT ROUND UP

Now you have reached the end of this chapter you should have plenty of positive ideas about how you can get the look you want. By now you should have become more active, started to look at the way you eat and be making the most of your clothes. Remember, you are *not* trying to turn yourself into a film star, you are trying to make the most of *you*. Check the following statements:

> ☐ I have the motivation to change my image.
>
> ☐ I am happy that the way I look reflects the way I want to be.

CHAPTER ELEVEN
LIVING A LONG AND HEALTHY LIFE

You owe it to yourself to look after your health. After all, getting what you want is going to do you no good if you are not there to enjoy it. In this chapter, you will learn how you can boost your health to give you both the stamina to go for what you want and the strength to withstand setbacks. Ideally, we all want to live a long life as well as a healthy one – though this partly lies in our genes. So you will learn how exercising, eating a healthy diet and paying attention to keeping your brain active can help you stay fit and active for as long as you live – however long that may be. You will also learn about the essential health checks you should have throughout life to help ensure you stay fit and well. As always, the stepwise plan with which you are now very familiar will help you. Just to jog your memory:

> Step one: Get in touch with your dream
>
> Step two: Research your dream
>
> Step three: Think out your plan of action
>
> Step four: Put your plan into action
>
> Step five: Check your progress

The first step, as always, is to tap into your dream. Imagine yourself in perfect health, with your body in perfect working order. Really visualise how it feels to be fit and healthy. How does it feel? Now project yourself into the future as an old person and imagine how you would like to be – still strong, active and with a lively brain. How does that feel? The good news is that you can get yourself into good physical shape. But first you need to know where you are, to identify your strengths and potential weaknesses so as to do what you can to maximise the former and counteract the latter.

HOW HEALTHY ARE YOU?

Now let's have a look at what your physical strengths and weaknesses are and how they might affect your health and longevity. You'll need a pen and a notebook.

Tick the ones that apply to you:

Smoking

- I have never smoked.
- I used to smoke but gave up.
- I smoke up to 20 cigarettes a day.
- I smoke 20–40 cigarettes a day.
- I smoke over 50 cigarettes a day.

Alcohol

- I drink more than 21 units a week (men).
- I drink more than 14 units of alcohol a week (women).

Exercise

- I exercise three or more times a week.
- I don't exercise regularly at all.

Weight

- I am five to ten pounds more than my ideal weight for my height.
- I am ten to 20 pounds more than my ideal weight for my height.
- I am 20–30 pounds more than my ideal weight for my height.
- I am more than 30 pounds more than my ideal weight for my height.

Food intake

- My meal times tend to be haphazard and irregular.
- I tend to eat a lot of snacks.
- I don't eat breakfast.
- I eat fewer than five helpings of fruit and vegetables a day.
- I enjoy fatty foods.
- I don't take multi-vitamin/mineral supplement.

Your genes

- One or more of my grandparents lived to be 80+.
- The average age my four grandparents lived to was:
  - 60–70 years.
  - 70–80 years.
  - 80 plus.
- My father or mother had a stroke or heart attack before age 50.
- Tick if any close relatives i.e. father, mother, grandparent, brother or sister, had any of the following before age 65:

- High blood pressure.
- Cancer.
- Heart disease.
- Stroke.
- Diabetes.
- Genetically transmitted disease.

How did you get on? Your personal potential for living a long and healthy life is a matter of balancing the minus points such as parents or grandparents who died at a young age, or had one of the illnesses mentioned before 65, and smoking, against the plus points you can accrue for yourself by eating a healthy diet, taking regular exercise and giving up smoking. The things you can't change are your genetic make-up and your family history. But that leaves plenty of areas of your life where you can make a real difference to your health. Use your answers to the quiz to construct a plan of action for yourself along the lines you are now familiar with. To get you started, let's have a look at just one area of increasing your fitness – exercise – in more detail.

HOW FIT ARE YOU?

Fitness doesn't just depend on how many games of tennis or step classes you do a week; it is also a question of how active you are in your normal everyday life. As with any plan to get what you want, your personal fitness campaign must start from where you are. You'll need a pen and a notebook.

Tick the ones that apply to you:

Time spent in a normal day walking about:
- Very little.
- Less than a quarter.

- A quarter to a half.
- Over half.

I carry objects (bags of shopping, children, crates or boxes, books, etc) heavier than 6.3 kg (14lb):

- Seldom.
- Up to five times a day.
- Six to 20 times a day.
- Over 20 times a day.

Most of my normal day:

- Is inactive.
- Involves light physical activity.
- Involves heavy physical activity.
- Is very strenuous.

Number of hours a week I walk or cycle:

- Less than one.
- One to two.
- Two to four.
- Over four.

Number of hours a week I spend in light physical activity e.g. gardening, hiking, social tennis:

- Less than two.
- Two to three.
- Three to four.
- Over four.

> Number of hours spent in vigorous physical activity e.g. squash, dancing, swimming, singles badminton or tennis:
> - Less than one.
> - Two to three.
> - Three to four.
> - Over four.
>
> I run up the stairs:
> - Seldom.
> - Sometimes.
> - Often.
> - Usually.
>
> I have had a baby:
> - In the last three to six months.
> - Less than three months ago.

How did you get on? Don't blame yourself if you didn't score very well. After all, today's lifestyles don't provide us with many opportunities to be active. In fact, the National Fitness Survey published in 1992 showed that seven out of ten men and eight out of ten women were not active enough to stay healthy. From now on you won't be one of them, because you are going to plan your own personal fitness campaign.

THINK OUT YOUR PLAN OF ACTION

The first step is to work out some goals and the time to start is right away. Simply by becoming more active in your daily life you will be taking the first step to a healthier, more vibrant you. Take the stairs instead of a lift, walk to the shops rather than taking the bus. Set yourself two targets for being more active. You should be active enough to get slightly out of breath at least once a day.

> Two ways in which I aim to become more active:
> 1 ....
> 2 ....

HARNESS YOUR IMAGINATION

Now you have started to become more active, start planning some more specific exercise, sport or activity. As always, the key to getting what you want is to visualise. Think about what exercises or activities you enjoyed or were good at in the past. Was there any sport or game you enjoyed when you were at school? If you were always first to plead a headache or your period when it was time for hockey or swimming, were there any other activities you enjoyed? Include things you may have done in your leisure time or on holiday. What about the time you went windsurfing with your friends on that Greek beach 'just for a giggle' — didn't you rather enjoy it? How about the time a friend persuaded you to go horseriding? Is there any particular sport or activity which you like watching?

Spend some time visualising what sports or activities appeal to you. Get into the fantasy, feel the wind through your hair as you skim over the waves on a sailboard, hear the beat and imagine your partner's body as you boogie across the dance floor, hear the applause as you take the centre court at Wimbledon.

Use visualisation to enhance your motivation when you have embarked on an exercise programme too. Breathe slowly and calmly as you imagine yourself performing your chosen activity, feel the emotions and sensations linked to your activity and imagine yourself getting stronger, feeling fitter and looking better.

Now think about doing some of those things for real. Choose three to investigate. Use the skills you have now acquired to set yourself goals and targets, marshall your resources and find out who can help you.

> Activities/sports I am going to investigate:
>
> 1 ....
>
> 2 ....
>
> 3 ....
>
> What skills do you need to develop in order to take up the activity of your choice?

The adage that you should 'Get fit to play squash, not play squash to get fit' is quite true, and the same goes for many other types of exercise or sports. In the early days of exercising it may be a good idea to take up something which you can do without needing a high level of skill, such as cycling, walking or running to build up your fitness.

KEEPING UP THE MOTIVATION

Check back on the motivators listed in the last chapter if you need any more encouragement. And just in case those aren't enough consider that exercise helps keep your heart beating strongly and strengthens your bones, so you are less likely to suffer from the brittle bone disease, osteoporosis, as you get older. Another way to keep up your motivation is to vary the exercise you do by what is called cross-training – doing several different activities. Another benefit of cross-training is it also helps protect against repetitive strain injuries caused by working the same part of the body and makes for better all-round fitness and shape.

EASY WAYS TO EXERCISE

Are you aware of any barriers that are preventing you from exercising? How about those old familiars: 'I haven't the time' and 'I can't afford it'? Here are some ideas to combat them.

- Get up early and go to the gym or exercise to an exercise video.

- Get off the bus or train two or three stops earlier than you need to and walk briskly the rest of the way.
- Jog/swim/go to a gym in your lunch hour.
- Go for a run when you get home after work.
- Walk to a local park in your lunch hour and walk back.
- Cycle to work.
- Park the car 20 minutes away from the office and walk briskly to work.
- If you have children and the school is not too far away, walk them to school.
- Invest in an exercise bike or rowing machine and do your exercise while you watch the news.

CHECK IT OUT

Once you are putting your fitness plan into action, don't forget to check on your progress. Every four weeks monitor your progress by doing the fitness checks, or having a fitness assessment at the gym. Plan your activity programme week by week, using the following diary:

> **My fitness diary**
>
> Sunday Monday Tuesday Wednesday Thursday Friday Saturday
>
> Activity:..
>
> Exercise: ....
>
> Fitness
> assessment: ....

Remember: exercise should be enjoyable not a grisly battle to keep fit.

STAYING HEALTHY

EATING FOR A LONG HEALTHY LIFE

As well as exercising, think about what you are putting into your body. You've already read some tips in the last chapter. Here are a few more:

- Fresh fruit and vegetables are one of the most important factors in living a long and healthy life. Anti-oxidant vitamins C, E and beta-carotene have been found to help reduce the risk of diseases such as heart disease, cancer and cataracts in later life. As many as 35% of cancers could be linked to diet. Minerals are important too: iron to prevent anaemia, calcium for strong bones and magnesium for energy.

- Step up your calcium. Calcium is vital for strong healthy bones. Your 20s are the years when you reach peak bone mass. The higher this is, the lower your risk of developing osteoporosis in later life. You need three to four servings of calcium-rich foods a day. Good sources are: low-fat milk and cheese, canned fish with bones, nuts and seeds, calcium-fortified products.

- Folic acid is vital, especially if you are planning a baby. It helps to prevent defects of the central nervous system, such as spina bifida. Good sources are: leafy green vegetables, fortified bread and cereals. The UK government now recommends that women planning a pregnancy, and those in the first 12 weeks of a pregnancy, should take a folic acid supplement of 400 microgrammes a day.

STAY ALERT, STAY YOUNG

Don't just assume that you have to slow down mentally as you get older. In fact, exercising your mental muscles is just as important as exercising your physical ones. It's now known that using your brain stimulates powerful brain chemicals called nerve growth factors, which will actually help the brain cells to send out new connections right into our 90s.

VITAL HEALTH CHECKS AT EVERY AGE

As well as taking responsibility for your health through watching your diet and exercising, you should also have regular health checks so that any potential problems can be spotted and sorted out early. Caring for your health is a way of showing that you care for yourself. So make a note in your long-term diary and check out the following:

- Well-person check (every two years)
  A well-person check-up can pinpoint areas of health to which you should pay special attention. Most GPs do such checks as part of their health promotion activities, so book an appointment. The doctor will want to know about any aspects of your lifestyle that could affect your health, including your job, the amount of exercise you do, and any habits that might put you at a higher risk of serious illness such as smoking or heavy alcohol consumption. You'll also be asked about your family medical history. Genetic factors play a part in heart disease, diabetes, osteoporosis and certain cancers, such as breast and bowel cancer (see 'Do you need special tests?', page 177).

- Cholesterol count
  If you have a family history of early heart disease or high cholesterol the doctor may recommend testing your cholesterol level. If you have a high count you'll be advised on diet and lifestyle changes to reduce your risk. If your level is very high you may be referred to a Lipid (blood fat) Clinic at the hospital, where cholesterol-lowering drugs may be prescribed.

- Blood pressure test (every two years)
  High blood pressure can start as early as your 20s and, if not detected, can lead to a higher risk of stroke and heart disease in later life. The Pill sometimes increases blood pressure, so it

should usually be checked whenever you renew your Pill prescription. If it is raised, you may need to take medication.

- Skin cancer self-examination (every three months)
Cases of skin cancer have risen dramatically in the past 20 years. Take ten minutes to check yourself over and get a friend or family member to check your back and any areas that aren't easily visible. A tan is your body's attempt to defend itself against sun damage. Sunbathing causes early ageing and if you're a sun worshipper you may already notice your skin showing signs of dryness, wrinkles and freckling now. Melanoma (the most serious kind of skin cancer) often arises from sunburn damage in childhood or the teens, so keep an eye out for suspicious signs. If you have children make sure they are protected against the sun, and keep young babies out of direct sunlight altogether.

- Dental check-up (every six months)
However diligent you are, brushing and flossing can't keep your teeth completely free of the plaque and tartar that cause gum disease and tooth loss. So see the dentist regularly.

- Eye test (as needed)
12 million people in the UK are short-sighted. If you wear glasses your optician (optometrist) will tell how often you should have your eyes tested. Others can request an eye test for specific problems such as difficulties with vision and frequent headaches.

FOR WOMEN ONLY

- Well-woman check (every three years)
Most GPs and some hospitals or family planning centres hold special well-woman clinics. Contraception is high on the agenda during your fertile years and though the Pill continues to be the most popular method, don't forget the other choices. Barrier methods (condoms and caps) in particular help prevent

sexually transmitted diseases, including HPV, the wart virus linked to cervical cancer. Using a condom protects you from HIV, the virus that causes AIDS.

- Cervical smear (every three years)
  This is vital if you've ever been sexually active and is included in the well-woman check. You're entitled to a smear every three years, though some women need one more often, and in some areas the interval between tests is five years. A few cells are removed from the cervix (the neck of the womb) and analysed for pre-cancerous changes. If you have a positive smear – and around one in 10 women do – this does not mean you have cancer. More often than not the cause is a minor abnormality which needs no further treatment. If a smear does show pre-cancerous changes you may be referred for a colposcopy. This involves looking at the cervix with a special instrument to see where the changes are. Several simple treatments can be done on an out-patient basis to prevent cells becoming cancerous.

- Breast examination
  The doctor or nurse can teach you how to examine your breasts. 'Breast cancer is extremely rare below 50,' says Oxford GP Dr Sally Hope. Most breast lumps before this age are benign (non-cancerous) and easily treatable. However, familiarity with your breasts can enable you to spot any suspicious changes as you get older, so this is one habit to start early.

Do the breast check!

- Stand in front of a mirror, hands at your sides, and check for dimpling, puckering, changes in the appearance of the skin, lumps and bumps, and any unusual nipple discharge. Repeat with hands on your hips and above your head.

- Now check your breasts by feeling them one at a time. Use the pads of your fingers and move them in small circles around each breast in turn, starting at the outer edge and

> working inwards towards the nipples. Feel your entire breast including under your armpit and up to your collarbone.
>
> - If you do feel a lump or notice any change, check the other breast to see if there is one like it – it could be a gland or a rib. If you find anything that wasn't there last month, see the doctor. Don't become obsessed with checking your breasts – remember nine out of ten lumps aren't cancer.

- Mammography (three-yearly after age 50)
  Women between 50 and 65 are eligible for mammograms (breast X-rays). You need to be referred to a breast clinic by your GP. Once registered, if all is well you'll be recalled every three years until you're 65. Your first mammograph will show two aspects of your breasts, and will be examined by two experts, for greater accuracy. It doesn't hurt but it may be a little uncomfortable. Even if you are recalled for further assessment remember that most abnormalities are not cancer. You should still continue to examine your breasts once a month, as most tumours are picked up by women themselves.

- Conception
  Half of all women in their 20s conceive within four months of trying and 70% within eight months. See the doctor if you've been trying for 18 months without success.

FOR MEN ONLY

While women are bombarded with information about health matters, most men are amazingly ignorant about the workings of their bodies. If you are a man, check out the following:

- Bones
  Over 10,000 men a year break a bone in their backs and 12,000 suffer hip fractures due to osteoporosis. In men, low levels of the

male hormone testosterone (hypogonadism), long courses of steroids for rheumatoid arthritis and asthma, and too much alcohol (more than 21 units a week – about 10½ pints of beer) are risk factors. The usual culprits – lack of exercise, a diet poor in calcium and smoking – can push up the risk too.

ACTION! Do weight–bearing exercises (e.g. running, walking, working with weights) three times a week and eat calcium-rich foods such as cheese, yoghurt, milk and green leafy vegetables.

- Heart

Seven out of eight men have a major risk factor for cardiovascular disease such as being overweight, having high blood pressure or high cholesterol level, lack of exercise, smoking or a family history of heart problems.

ACTION! Switch from fry-ups to grills, eat more fresh fruit and vegetables, cut down on the booze, and try to kick the weed. Cutting back on salt and increasing calcium lowers blood pressure. Red wine protects against heart disease – but you should stick to under 21 units (glasses) a week. Walking two or three miles a day protects against death from heart attack, so walk to the station. You should visit the GP every couple of years for routine checks on blood pressure, weight and cholesterol level.

- Stomach

Over half of all men weigh more than they should and 13% are so overweight that their health is at risk. Yet, most men don't pay attention to what they eat and some even seem proud of their pot-bellies. Fat distribution is a risk factor for heart disease – apple-shaped men, who carry weight around the waistline, have higher cholesterol levels and are greater risk of heart attacks and strokes.

ACTION! Eat five portions of fresh fruit and vegetables a day. These are rich in anti-oxidant vitamins C, E and beta-carotene, which help combat heart disease. Oily fish, like salmon, herring and sardines contain essential fatty acids to help lower cholesterol and keep the arteries unclogged.

- Penis
  Sperm counts have halved in the last fifty years and in couples with infertility the male factor has risen from one in ten to one in four. Pesticides, food additives and other chemicals have all been blamed. Lack of exercise, excess weight, poor diet and alcohol can all damage sperm production.
  ACTION! Sperm are healthier if the testicles are kept cool, so wear boxer shorts and avoid saunas and hot baths. Avoid heavy drinking and smoking, eat healthily and make love two or three times a week if you are trying for a baby.

- Impotence
  Nearly half of all men have periods of impotence, but only one in ten confess the problem to their GPs. Six out of ten men have an underlying medical problem such as diabetes or arterial disease. Other culprits include alcohol, smoking and diseases of the nervous system such as multiple sclerosis. Low levels of the male hormone testosterone is a factor for three out of a hundred men.
  ACTION! Avoiding penetrative sex and concentrating on other ways of showing your love for each other is often all that's needed to restore confidence – and an erection. If the problem is more deep-seated, there's now a drug which is very successful.

- Testes
  The risk of developing testicular cancer – the most common cancer in men aged 15 to 49 – has doubled in the last 25 years. Men who exercise regularly are less likely to develop it, possibly because exercise can alter hormonal balance.
  ACTION! Get into the habit of examining your testicles regularly. It's easiest to do after a bath or shower when you are warm and relaxed. Feel each testicle between fingers and thumb of both hands. Any change, such as a hardening, swelling or lump should be reported to the doctor.

- Prostate
  2.4 million British men, especially those over 50, suffer enlarged prostate – benign prostatic hypertrophy (BPH). Although it is

harmless, it can cause problems such as having to rush to the toilet, a feeling of not emptying the bladder properly, dribbling urine, bladder infections and retention of urine (inability to pass water). More seriously, deaths from prostate cancer, the third commonest male cancer, have risen in the last ten years. Japanese men are ten times less likely to develop it – perhaps because their diets are healthier.

ACTION! Eat less animal fat, more fruit and vegetables and lose excess weight. If you have trouble passing water, see the doctor.

DO YOU NEED SPECIAL TESTS?

You may need more frequent check-ups and to take special measures to ensure you stay fit and well if you have a family history or specific risk factors which predispose you towards certain diseases:

- Breast cancer
  Risk factors:
  - Close female relatives (mother or sister) who had the disease before age 50, especially if the disease was in both breasts.
  - Started your periods early and menopause late.
  - Had children after the age of 30.

  ACTION! Ask your GP about genetic counselling and go for regular ultrasound scans of your breasts and mammography before age 50.

- Cervical cancer
  Risk factors:
  - Previous HPV infection or pre-cancerous changes which have needed a colposcopy.
  - Smoking.
  - If you, or your partner, has had a lot of sexual partners.

  ACTION! Try not to smoke, use a barrier contraceptive, and if you've had previous HPV infection or pre-cancerous changes go for more frequent smears.

- Skin cancer
  Risk factors:
  - Family history.
  - Fair-skin, blue eyes, red or blond hair and freckles.
  - A tendency to burn rather than tan.
  - Moles.
  - Early exposure to strong sunlight during childhood or youth.

  ACTION! Protect yourself in the sun. Make regular checks. Report any persistent rough patches or irregular, slowly growing lumps, sores, or moles, or any changes in a wart or mole, such as bleeding or itching, to your doctor.

- Ovarian cancer
  Risk factors:
  - Family history of breast or ovarian cancer.
  - No children.

  ACTION! The combined contraceptive pill protects against the disease, as does pregnancy. Vaginal ultrasound can help detect early cancers.

- Heart disease
  Risk factors:
  - Family history of heart disease before 55 on your father's side or 65 on your mother's side.
  - High blood pressure (over 140/90).
  - Overweight.
  - Smoking.
  - Diabetes.

  ACTION! Pay attention to your lifestyle and ask your doctor about referring you to a specialist in case you need more active treatment for high levels of cholesterol or high blood pressure.

LIVING A LONG AND HEALTHY LIFE ROUND UP

So now you know how to make an action plan that should ensure you stay as healthy as you can for as long as you can. Don't forget to check your progress from time to time and to revisit your plan and set new goals from time to time. Before you go on to the next chapter check out the following statements:

> ☐ I am aware of my own personal potential for health.
>
> ☐ I am determined to eat to stay healthy.
>
> ☐ I intend to commit myself to a regular exercise programme.
>
> ☐ I will take responsibility for having regular health checks.
>
> ☐ I deserve to stay healthy.
>
> ☐ I am committed to staying healthy.

Ready? Then it's almost time for us to part company. By now, you should be well on the way to getting what you want and, as a result, be feeling happier and more fulfilled than ever before. So now let's see what else you can do.

CHAPTER TWELVE
IT'S YOUR LIFE

This chapter is one of the shortest in *How To Get What You Want*, yet it is also one of the most important. It's all about personal growth, or fulfilling your own potential. The reason it is so short is that the whole of *How To Get What You Want* has been about looking at ways in which you can grow and develop.

Personal growth means becoming aware of your own potential and that of others around you. It's about developing yourself in every area of your life, so you become a whole, healthy person. It includes looking at your relationships and learning how to manage them, learning to listen to the messages of your body, learning to use all parts of your brain. Above all, it means taking charge and living your life as you want to live it.

> Have a look at the following statements and tick the ones that apply to you:
>
> - I feel able to praise others and am able to accept praise in turn for a job well done
> - I feel able encourage others in their endeavours
> - I accept and appreciate myself and other people
> - I am consistent and reliable in my dealings with others
> - I expect to succeed at things I set out to do

- I trust myself to carry out my own intentions and those of others
- I respect myself and other people
- I don't feel threatened if others are different from me

GETTING IN TOUCH WITH YOUR SPIRITUAL NEEDS

Personal growth, then, is all about looking at your wants and needs and taking responsibility for meeting them. Those needs and wants don't just include the physical and mental needs that we have looked at elsewhere. They also include the needs of your soul or spirit, call it what you like. Some people choose to satisfy these by turning to some sort of formal religion, by taking up New Age philosophy, through relaxation or meditation, by immersing themselves in the world of nature or a piece of art. Others get involved in personal development work or some sort of humanistic psychology. This may include sharing experiences in a group with others who are also in search of their 'higher self'. The way you choose is entirely up to you. But, however you choose to cater for your spiritual needs, you should spend some time thinking about developing your own personal philosophy. Here are some suggestions:

- Go on a retreat.
- Meditate or pray (if you are religious).
- Get out into nature: mountains, lakes and the sea are all spiritually uplifting.
- Focus on a piece of art: painting, poetry, music.
- Tune into the world of your dreams and imagination.
- Explore therapy, psychoanalysis or personal development work.
- Get involved in religion, rituals, ceremony.

MONITORING YOUR PERSONAL GROWTH

Your personal growth is not something that ever stops. It continues throughout your life as you have new experiences and learn from them. It means learning to listen to your feelings and your body and to trust the wisdom of your mind. Have a look at the following checklist, based on one devised by US psychologist Robert E. Alberti, and fill in the ones that apply to you.

1. Expanding your horizons
   In the last week/month/three months/six months/year:
   - A new sport or game I have participated in is ....
   - An important issue I have changed my views on is
   - A new hobby/leisure pursuit I have taken up is .....
   - A new field I have taken a course in is..................
   - A different language/culture I have explored is .....
   - I have paid attention to my body and feelings in the following ways ....
   - I have tried the following new cuisine....................
   - I have listened to the following new music ....
   - I have smelt the following new smell......................
   - I have allowed myself to cry/laugh until I cried/say 'I love you'/scream at the top of my voice/admit I was afraid ....
   - I have watched the sun or moon rise or set/a bird soar/a flower open to the sun...................................
   - I have travelled to the following new place ....
   - I have made a new friend/nurtured an old friendship ....

- I have spent an hour or more really talking and listening to the following person from a different background (culture, race, gender, class, religion). ....
- I have allowed my imagination to roam freely for 10 minutes to an hour or more..................................

2. Living for today
   In the last week/month/three months/six months/year:

   - I have done the following thing I really wanted to do, without letting fear of the consequences hold me back ....
   - I have stopped to 'listen' to what my body was telling me ....
   - I have expressed my anger, joy, fear, sadness spontaneously without thinking about it........................
   - I have done the following thing I wanted to do, rather than something I felt I ought to do ....
   - I have allowed myself to spend time or money on the following thing that gave me pleasure now rather than saving for tomorrow......................................
   - I have bought the following thing I wanted on impulse ....
   - I have done the following thing no-one (including myself) expected me to do..................................

3. Trusting yourself
   In the last week/month/three months/six months/year:

   - On the following occasion I did what I felt was right against the advice of other people........................
   - On the following occasion I experimented with new solutions to old problems....................................

- On the following occasion I stood up for my own views in the face of disapproval..
- On the following occasion I used my own intellectual reasoning to work out a solution to a thorny problem. ....
- On the following occasion I made a decision and acted on it straight away..
- On the following occasion I acted in a way that showed that I believe in my ability to direct my own life..........
- I cared enough about myself to have the following regular health checks (see previous chapter)..............
- On the following occasion I told other people about my personal philosophy of life.......................................
- On the following occasion I assumed a position of leadership in my work, an organisation or other group ....
- On the following occasion I stood up for myself when I thought I was being treated unfairly.........................
- On the following occasion I risked sharing my feelings with another person ....
- On the following occasion I designed/built/made/created something of my own ....
- On the following occasion I admitted I was wrong......

Just by reading this book and following your *How To Get What You Want* campaign will have ensured that you ticked lots of things. Use your checklist to suggest other ways you can grow and develop and keep a regular check to make sure that you continue to do so throughout life. Before we finally part company, the next chapter shows you what you can do if you *don't* get what you want.

IT'S YOUR LIFE ROUND UP

This chapter has been concerned with your personal growth, which by its very nature is very individual and unique to you. The following checklist is inevitably less precise than those of previous chapters. Use it to help you keep your own personal development needs in mind:

- [ ] I am committed to giving time and attention to my need for personal growth and development.
- [ ] I feel more in touch with my spiritual needs.
- [ ] I trust myself to do what is right for me and to follow my own path throughout life.

CHAPTER THIRTEEN
YOU CAN'T ALWAYS GET WHAT YOU WANT

Throughout this book, you have learnt about many different ways of getting what you want, but, however much you try, there will be some occasions on which you don't reach your dreams. Sometimes outside factors over which you have no control may conspire against you; at other times you will play a part. It is human to make mistakes, so don't make matters worse by beating yourself over the head. Perhaps your goals weren't thought out clearly enough, perhaps they were not, after all, realistic, perhaps you didn't have the right skills or talents, or perhaps, having got what you thought you wanted, you realised that it wasn't what you wanted at all.

This chapter is all about how to cope when things go wrong. In it, you will discover some ways to cope with your disappointment, how to get the support you need from other people, and how to look after yourself in the down times. You will also learn how to look at your original plan and analyse the points at which it went wrong.

DEALING WITH YOUR EMOTIONS

Before you can do anything else you need to deal with your emotional reactions to your disappointment. If you don't, you may end up becoming stuck and embittered, unable to move on to the next challenge.

Disappointment can take many forms: you may feel an overwhelming grief that things didn't work out as you planned; anger that your plans have been thwarted; fear at what the future now holds; or guilt at the thought that something you did was responsible or at having involved others in a plan that failed. Such feelings are natural, but if you are to learn from your experience and move on, they must be dealt with.

The very first step is to acknowledge that you are feeling them. Many of us have been brought up to think that our feelings, especially negative ones such as anger, guilt, sorrow or fear, are childish – 'Big boys don't cry' – or shameful – 'You should be ashamed to shout like that, a big girl like you.' The result is that it can sometimes be hard to acknowledge and accept our feelings. Many of us bury our true emotions or hide them under a veil of more acceptable ones. For example, we appear bored or embarrassed when we are really afraid, tense when we are angry, argumentative or cocky when deep down we feel guilty.

Each one of us experiences emotions in a different way. When I feel angry I experience an unbearable feeling of pressure in my head until I feel I will explode. When I am sad, the whole world seems dull, as if it has lost its colour. When I am afraid, I experience a tight feeling in my chest, shaking legs, and the desire to run anywhere as fast as I can. In order to deal with your feelings you must learn to recognise what they feel like.

How do you feel when you experience the following? Write down the answers in as much detail as you can thinking about what you feel, hear, see, smell, even taste.

- When I am angry I feel ....
- When I am afraid I feel ....
- When I am guilty I feel ....
- When I am disappointed I feel ....
- When I am sad I feel ....
- When I am happy I feel ....
- When I am elated I feel ....

> - Think of any other emotions and write down how you feel
> ....

How do you feel now? Doing this exercise should have given you the confidence to know that you can identify and name your feelings. Don't worry if you didn't find it that easy – most of us aren't used to being emotionally literate. But from now on, try to identify what you are feeling and name your feelings.

Your next step is to deal with your emotions. As with everything, there are several choices:

- You can express them in words. For example, 'I'm feeling irritated'; 'I'm in a lousy temper'; 'I'm very upset'; 'I'm really scared.'
- You can express them physically by allowing yourself to cry, shout, scream, quake, curl into a ball.
- You can release and discharge them by doing something else such as digging the garden, tidying the house, going for a swim, having a hard game of tennis or whatever.
- You can transform them into something else by using them to create something – a piece of writing, a painting, a musical composition.
- You can control them by repressing or suppressing them.

There may be times when you need to take the last option. You may need to 'keep a stiff upper lip' on some occasions, either for your own sake to help you cope or for the sake of others. Suppressing your feelings of grief when someone has died, for example, may allow you to do something else which requires you to be cool and level-headed, such as talking to the solicitor. However, on the whole, sweeping your emotions under the carpet for any length of time isn't terribly healthy and can sometimes mean that they re-emerge at a later stage.

So, if you are feeling disappointed, find a place where you feel safe and allow your emotions full rein and express them in various ways. Now you are aware of how you can deal with your emotions, it's time to list some of the specific things you might choose to do in your notebook.

SEND IN THE TROOPS

Emotions can often feel overwhelming, so you will also need support from other people: your friends, partner, children, relatives. Support can be anything from a smile to praise or appreciation. Not all the people in your life will be capable (or willing) of giving you the support you need. They may find it difficult to deal with their own emotions and so feel embarrassed or ill at ease with yours, they may be busy with their own concerns, or it may simply be the wrong time. Rather than feeling resentful, try to obtain your support from a variety of people. Some of the people in your life may be better at giving practical support – making you a meal, cleaning the house or tidying your desk. Others will be good at listening – providing a shoulder to cry on, hearing you out as you explain for the fiftieth time how if only you had been willing to have another child your partner wouldn't have walked out. Others will be good at helping you to work out where things went wrong – challenging your beliefs and attitudes, helping you feel more energetic and positive. Others may simply be relaxing to be around. These are some of the people I know I can turn to in times of trouble:

- My friend Chris – logical discussion, suggesting distractions.
- My friend Jane – understanding, sympathy, long phone calls.
- My daughter Kate – making me cups of tea/bringing me meals/encouraging chats/hugs.
- My daughter Lucy – discussing emotions/talking on the phone/sending me homemade cards/coming to see me.
- My friend Nigel – making me laugh.
- My friend Ricky – giving me encouragement.
- My bank manager – lending me money (sometimes!): and so on . . .

Now it's time for you to list your support troops. Make a list of all the people you can call on in times of trouble and write in the type of support they are able to offer.

LOOKING AFTER YOURSELF

Support doesn't just have to come from other people, it can also come from you. Learning to care for yourself and knowing that you are able to support yourself can be tremendously empowering. It allows you to feel that even in your darkest hour, you are still in control of your life. Supporting yourself means being kind to yourself, treating yourself as you would a friend who was in trouble. Learn to like and love yourself, to value what you have to offer yourself, to appreciate the wisdom you have gained simply by living up until now. Part of supporting yourself involves looking after your body (you've already seen how in Chapters Ten and Eleven) not just when you are under duress but every day, so it has the power to support you physically when you are undergoing mental pain.

Another part of supporting yourself involves learning to tune into your emotions (see above) and trusting the wisdom of your mind, body and spirit. Use your mind to analyse what went wrong (more of this below). Use the creative part of your brain to think about what went wrong. Keep a diary (I always do). Write a letter to someone you feel angry with (keep it – and then tear it up). Talk yourself out of negative emotions (see the section on the loser mentality in Chapter Seven) and give yourself encouragement. Here are some messages you can use:

- Many people love me
- I love myself
- I have some happy memories I can call on
- I am free to live my own life
- I don't need to feel guilty
- I will not make the same mistake again
- I can let go of the past

Now think of some of your own.

Supporting yourself also means knowing what things you can *do* to distract, support, heal or ease your distress. These things don't have to be expensive or time-consuming (unless you want them to be). Learn to tune into simple things that give you pleasure. These are some of the things I do when I'm feeling miserable:

- Phone a friend or my sister.
- Write a letter to someone who loves me.
- Write in my diary.
- Listen to some classical music.
- Put on a salsa tape and dance round my sitting-room.
- Go out for a walk.
- Look through my holiday snaps or stick photos in my photo album.
- Light some candles and run myself a bath scented with aromatherapy oils.

The list could go on. But now it's your turn. Try the following exercise.

> 1. Draw a picture of yourself in the middle of a large piece of paper – make it as realistic or unrealistic as you like.
>
> 2. All around you, draw in the things that help you when you are feeling blue – pets, work, exercise, music, books, friends, family, holidays and so on.

Does it make you feel better? Now you know that you can support yourself if you need it.

IT'S NOT THE END OF THE WORLD

Even though it might seem as if your whole world has caved in when things go wrong, with time you will come to realise that what has happened isn't a catastrophe, unless you let it be. We can't always succeed in getting what we want. It's natural to feel down-hearted when things don't work out in the way you had hoped. Yet, once you have emerged from them, you will be able to look at what you have gained. The end of a relationship, the loss of your job, discovering that, after all, you didn't have enough talent to become a concert pianist are all sad, yes, and you need to mourn the loss of your hopes and dreams. However, once you have done so, it's time to look forward. Every ending brings a new beginning: the end of a relationship gives you the chance to try and find someone better suited to you; the loss of a job, the chance to look for one that uses your skills and talents to better advantage; the end of your ambition to be a concert pianist leaves you free to enjoy playing the piano purely for pleasure, without the pressure to perform.

LOOKING TOWARDS THE FUTURE

Now you have dealt with your emotions it's time to look at what went wrong so you can learn from your experience and move on – in other words it's time to engage your brain. Whenever you don't get what you want it's time to go back to the drawing board and look at your original plan. Ask yourself the following questions:

- Were my goals the right ones for the plan? Were they too big, too small, too unspecific, unrealistic?
- What barriers were there in my way? Did they come from other people or circumstances? Or did they come from within me?
- What have I learnt from this experience? What was good about it? What was bad about it?

Now you have some answers it's time to consider your dream and, if necessary, start again. There are four things you can do when something goes wrong:

- Try to change the existing situation. This is usually the first strategy most of us consider: arrange to alter your working hours, tell your partner you want to go out together at least one night a week, ask other people to change what they do and so on. Basically, it means examining the choices you have in the situation you are in and then choosing some different ones.

- Abandon ship. This is the most drastic solution, but if you feel you have exhausted all your other options it may be the only one left to you, so leave your job, your lover, your house, your problem.
- Change yourself. This is what this book has been all about so by now you have had plenty of practice. Use the skills you have learnt to create a new dream, change your attitude, behaviour, lifestyle, or whatever else is in your power.
- Learn to live with it. This option isn't as negative as it sounds, so long as you make it an active decision. Take control and work out how you can play down the bad parts of your situation – for example by investing more energy in leisure activities if you are unhappy at work, by finding other ways of meeting the needs your partner doesn't satisfy, if you are in an unhappy relationship and so on.

YOU CAN'T ALWAYS GET WHAT YOU WANT ROUND UP

In this chapter you have learnt that, though you can't always get what you want, you don't have to sink into a slough of despond. You can cope when bad things happen (for more on how to do this see my book *The Survivor Personality*). Now it's almost time for us to part company. But first look at the list and tick the following statements:

☐ I am confident that I know how to identify and express my emotions.

☐ I know who I can turn to in times of trouble.

☐ I trust myself to give myself the support I need when I need it.

☐ I am aware of the things I can do to help myself.

☐ I am prepared to admit my mistakes and learn from them.

CHAPTER FOURTEEN
THIS IS JUST THE BEGINNING

Now we have finally reached the end of what has been a long and exciting journey, it's time to congratulate yourself. The road we have taken together hasn't always been easy, but I think you'll agree that – even if you haven't yet achieved everything you want – it's been both challenging and interesting. So congratulate yourself for getting this far and allow yourself to celebrate your achievements.

From now on you are on your own. However, the skills you have learnt throughout this book will always be there. Look after them, practise them, nurture them. From now on as you live each day think about the following:

> **1. Greet each day with love**
> Avoid leaping straight out of bed the moment you wake up if you can. Instead, take some time to welcome the day and the fact that you are alive. Whatever the weather, take the time to notice and appreciate it through your senses: the warmth of the sun and the blue of the sky in summer, the myriad different types of clouds and shades of grey in winter.
>
> **2. If at first you don't succeed, try again until you do**
> Succeeding at what you set out to do is a great self-esteem booster, so don't give up if you encounter setbacks. Try again,

or try something new. Congratulate yourself on your success in small endeavours too, not just the big goals you have set for yourself.

3. Think positive
Numerous research studies and books have shown the power of positive thinking in helping you feel strong and good about yourself. So banish those negative thoughts and keep focused on the positive.

4. Live each day as if it is your last
Living in the present, not regretting the past and not fearing the future, is seen as the key to happiness both in modern psychological theories and the ancient art of meditation. If you had no time left you would be forced to live in the present. If this were your last day on earth how would you want to live it? Who would you want to be there? What would you want to do? What food would you eat? What experiences would you especially savour? What people, things or experiences are especially precious? Your answers to these questions reflect your core values – the things you really want. Now try to incorporate these elements into your daily life.

5. Master your emotions
Allowing your feelings to rule you makes you feel weak and at their mercy. Mastering your emotions by understanding them and learning how, when and where to express them effectively puts you back in control. There are plenty of hints throughout this book on ways in which you can become the master not the slave of your emotions.

6. Learn to laugh
Laughter really is the best medicine. When we laugh we relax and forget our troubles, or at least learn to see them in their true perspective. Laughter, like exercise, meditation and relaxation, triggers the release of the body's natural 'feel good' hormones, endorphins. And it even exercises your

muscles. All good reasons to tune into the power of laughter. There are all sorts of ways you can inject more humour into your life. Take some trouble to find your favourite comedians and then capture them on video, or find some authors you like to read who have a quirky approach to life. Spend an evening with a friend who likes to laugh . . .

7. Use your talents, skills and assets to the full
Feeling that you are using your talents, skills and assets at home, at work and in your relationships is a tremendous source of satisfaction, so identify your talents and skills from small things like boiling an egg to major accomplishments like being a world expert on astrophysics and then give yourself opportunities to exercise them.

8. Plan your life
Thinking about what you want to do, whether it's on an hourly, daily, monthly, yearly or life-long basis gives you a sense of mastery and control that is tremendously calming. Learning to think ahead can help you to control crises and deal with them in the most effective way.

9. Be enthusiastic
An enthusisastic approach to life and other people pays dividends. Other people will warm to your enthusiasm. Enthusiasm helps give you the motivation to get things done, which in turn helps you to feel good about yourself. And enthusiasm gives you the power to keep going when things get rough. Find out what fires you up – it can be something as simple as playing peek-a-boo with your baby to a computer game – whatever turns you on. But once you have identified what makes you glow make sure that every day you do something – whether it's at work, at home or in play – that triggers your enthusiasm.

10. Have faith in yourself
Self-confidence can help you point yourself in the direction you want to go and keep you on the path to achieving

> whatever you want to achieve, whether the going is smooth or rough. Tell yourself: I can do it – really!

From now on you have the tools to put your dreams into action whatever you want and whenever you want it. Getting what you want is a process that goes on throughout your life. It starts with knowing yourself – and that's where it ends too. Let me leave you with a favourite quotation of mine from the poet T. S. Eliot:

> *We shall not cease from exploration*
> *And the end of all our exploring*
> *Will be to arrive where we started*
> *And know the place for the first time.*
>
> Four Quartets, Little Gidding

Thank you for sharing the exploration with me.

PART THREE
INSPIRATIONS

CHAPTER FIFTEEN
INSPIRING PEOPLE AND BOOKS

The following case histories illustrate how a variety of people got what they wanted, what inspired them, the barriers they had to overcome and how they got where they wanted to be. Some of them started off with few advantages, others with disadvantages, but all of them found something that suited them and pursued their goals until they got what they wanted. If they can do it, so can you.

- 'Leaving my marriage gave me the courage'
  Louise Faulkes, self-employed alternative therapist.

    Louise was aware that her teachers and family never believed she could achieve much. Leaving school she became a hairdresser, 'because I liked working with my hands'. After a while, she did an evening class and decided to enter advertising. One day she was called into the manager's office and told that the company was going to change and so must her attitude. She started to think about changing her life.

    This was a low spot in her life: her marriage was breaking up (she had got married with 'a silly unrealistic notion of what love was'), she did not like her job and she didn't like working purely for money. She thought, 'There has to be more to life than this.' She had no clear idea in her head but she knew she wanted change.

    Being a 'people person' as well as liking working with her hands she *decided to do a massage course in her spare time. It started as a hobby, but she discovered she had an aptitude. She took an exam and started doing one evening a week's massage at a local health club. It was around now, in her early 30s, when her marriage was about to end that she decided to leave her job. A few weeks later she obtained a job at a health club and has never looked back. She felt she was communicating with people, who were more real to her, and she was using her hands. Although she now believes her marriage could have been saved, she believes that leaving it was a powerful motivator. 'If I had stayed I would not have had the determination. It would have been too easy to stay in and curl up on the sofa.'*

Something that helped her achieve a direction in life was an 'enlightenment course' she went on when she split up with her husband. Before this her attitude was, 'This is your life, make the best of it.' After doing the course, she realised she had the power to change. As a result she attended a 'focus' course for careers. She knew she wanted a less intellectual career, more physical than mental, and this helped her focus on her success as a masseuse. She liked the fact she was using her hands and that she was in control.

She took further courses in reflexology, sports therapy, colour therapy, and a diploma in teaching massage, physiology and aromatherapy. After two years at the health club she became self-employed. This seemed like a natural move and gave her the opportunity to grow. She was no longer at the beck and call of others; it was her own decision whether she was capable or not. 'The sky was my limit.' She said, 'There is no motivation when you are employed by others – only money – now all successes and failures are mine.' She was more motivated than ever. Being self-employed made her work harder because it was no longer just a job but a way of life.

What has kept her going is 'my need to communicate and hating my talent to go to waste'. She is still achieving in her life and, despite being blind in one eye and fearing roads, recently passed her driving test. She is now doing a master's degree in therapeutic bodywork.

- 'My insecurity drives me on'
  James Herbert, author of horror novels

James Herbert's parents ran market stalls in the East End of London. He believes his poor background and insecurity were his main motivation to achieve. As a child, James was streetwise. He was brought up to work hard and survive. His dream was 'to get out and be successful'.

He liked art and wanted to achieve success in this field but felt he couldn't be a painter, so went into advertising. Money was 'a strong motivation', though he believes 'that is not as simple as it sounds'. 'Money in terms of success was a motivator because of my insecurity.' He was a successful art director for many years. He believes his East End might might have been a barrier but — remember this was the 1960s, the era of Michael Caine, David Bailey, Terence Stamp and the rest — it didn't hold him back.

James had no idea or dream that he wanted to write. He started because 'it seemed like a good idea at the time'. His motive was that he was 'exploding with ideas' which could not find expression in advertising. He always knew he could write and had always told stories. His novel, The Rats, was accepted straightaway and became very popular.

For five years, advertising was his career and writing his hobby. He never believed there was 'no time' and his insecurity about his background drove him on. Eventually, he gave up working in advertising for three reasons. He felt he was 'killing myself working all the time'. He felt his family was suffering because he never saw them. The third motivation was the taxman: he was effectively working for nothing because at this time he was paying 83% tax. He chose writing over advertising because his love is creativity and writing was 'a pure thing to do'. He said, 'With writing you are God on the page. You can paint pictures with words.' His success as a writer was not planned but evolved from an early direction in his life. He feels he was lucky not to have a choice about what he did: his talent was his only escape from his background.

He often gets tense, but he uses this, the adrenalin it creates, and his own feeling of inadequacy to inspire him to achieve more. What he writes is never as good as he wants it to be. He knows there is no such thing as perfection, but 'I know it can be better' and this motivates him.

He feels lucky to have had two bites of the cherry, achieving success as an art director and as an author, but he says, 'You can always improve and the more you set out to do the better you become.'

- 'Challenge and risk fire me up'
  Bill Bingham, company trouble shooter

Bill Bingham started his career in accountancy and gradually moved up the ladder until he established himself as a 'trouble shooter' for troubled companies. His motivation was getting bored easily and the realisation that he thrived on short-term challenge and risk rather than routine.

'I always pick the biggest challenge because risk comes along with achieving things.' He uses a three stage plan: 'In the first stage you have to learn about the company and establish its problems. In the second you have to make decisions and management solutions. In the third you have to make sure your plans are working accordingly and make any adjustments.' The rescue tends to follow a three-year cycle which for Bill is ideal, because 'it is a short-term job where things happen quickly, there is little routine and this makes it exciting'. Companies are usually troubled, not because of their employees, but because 'they do not believe in themselves', he says.

One of the biggest motivators is having control over how he works. He also likes being an outsider as 'if you are a company man you often have to give up what you have or put it on the line'. The most enjoyable – and challenging – task was rescuing a big US company: 'The odds were against them achieving success and it depended very much on public investment.' He feels optimism is important. 'It is easy when things do not go well to let depression feed on itself until things get worse.' Half the battle is 'believing things can work'. After succeeding at this job, at 46, he felt he had taken his biggest risk career-wise and personally. 'There was no where else to go,' so he decided to retire. 'I enjoy having time to play golf, but if another high risk came along I would probably take the challenge.'

- *'To be a DJ was my dream'*
  Marco Amaldi, DJ

Marco Amaldi was first aware of his interest in music when he was six years old. 'My mum always used to play music to me and my cousins when we were young to calm us down and entertain us.' From the age of eight he listened to the charts and taped his favourite songs from the radio. While other children were spending pocket money on toys he was buying singles. He started to make compilations of tapes from his favourite singles. His dream of becoming a DJ started when he went to a small underground music gig. His motivation and inspiration was 'the effect I witnessed/experienced music having on people. It is a ritual experience, something that links people from all walks of life to dance together and release the pressures of everyday life.'

Leaving school at 17, he gained a good job in recruitment, but he didn't abandon his dream. The money he earned all went on building up his record collection. At 24, he decided to leave to pursue his dream. These were hard times. Sometimes he would go without food so he could buy a record. 'To get by I used to swap records and built up a reputation with other DJs of being able to track down good tracks.' Selling records was hard for him but he tried to see it in a positive way: 'firstly it allowed me to keep my collection a manageable size — at one point my collection was so big it was hard to move in my room; secondly it helped me fund my career.' He managed to get a couple of summer DJing jobs abroad, but came back to England early because a DJ he admired was playing and he 'went for inspiration — to see how it was done properly'.

He started to play at parties on the beach, in houses and with other successful sound systems (people who work together under the same name). He also got involved in setting up small clubs with friends and selling tapes in markets. He began to get feedback and built up a name via his tapes. A disappointment was discovering that behind the scenes, the life of a DJ is not as glamorous as he dreamed. To overcome this, he concentrates on the effect his DJing has, as this is what 'I want to be there for'.

His first break came when he went to Glastonbury in 1992. Some friends who had set up a sound system asked him to do a spot of DJing at the last minute and he was approached by some club organisers in the audience who liked how he played. At last he began to earn a living out of DJing. His next big break came when he was asked to play regularly at a popular London club with a reputation as a platform for underground music. He is now working on records and hopes to produce an album.

- *'I'll stop when I hear, "Bill Hull – who's he?"'*
  Bill Hull, OBE and ISOMB, former diplomat.

Bill came from a working class family in Islington, North London. He describes himself as 'a natural scholar'. Though it was rare for someone with his background, at 10 he gained a scholarship to go to grammar school. From an early age he was aware of a strong sense of responsibility. Leaving school at 17 he joined the Navy. After the war he went in to the Colonial Office. He liked 'being part of a disciplined organisation'. He also wanted 'the opportunity to travel, which held the excitement and glamour of war – without the fear'.

In 1963 he moved to the Foreign Office as Britain was running out of territories to administer. This was a 'natural move' as he still wanted the opportunity to travel. He liked the fact that in these organisations 'you know where you stand' and he also liked the discipline. Bill feels his career and achievements 'evolved' rather than being strictly planned, but they weren't accidental either. The only barrier he ever encountered was the 'power' of those above him. This happened when he had set his heart on a job in the Colonial Office which he did not get. At the time he was very upset but did not make a fuss. It was only a few years later that he found out his colleagues had blocked him, when he overheard a conversation. He was grateful, as he felt they did know best, since the job he failed to get didn't develop into what he wanted. He said, 'It goes to show one does not always know what is best for one.'

Naturally extrovert and forthright, Bill says that he had to 'learn to sit and wait for others to come to me'. He had to become 'more delicate and responsive' to others too. These were skills he learnt to develop. Working in a relatively small organisation, he was able to 'play the system in the sense that you could "trim your sails", develop the necessary qualities, and everyone would know'. He felt he would not have progressed as far in a large organisation. He felt he had never made sacrifices for his career. He likes 'the loneliness of command', and this was compatible with his goals as a young boy: he wanted prestige, authority and an interesting life. His career offered 'reasonable financial rewards, success, I was in demand and received awards (OBE and ISOMB)'.

Despite what may seem like a glamorous life, Bill always kept his feet on the ground. He said, 'A lot of overseas life is tinsel and froth. You are given a big house and a big entertainment allowance,' but he was determined not to 'lose' himself. His roots are firmly planted and, in his permanent bases, he has not ventured far from where he grew up. Today he works for five consultancies, is the president of a few clubs and a member of many. He will stop work when he hears the words, 'Bill Hull – who's he?'

- 'A degree put me on equal terms with the professionals'
  Ros Barber

Ros left school with no qualifications. She spent the next few years working and travelling. She did well in sales and marketing (she held a good job with BMW). However, although she believed she was capable, she felt that her lack of formal qualifications was holding her back and did not have the confidence to pursue promotion.

After marrying at the age of 32, she gradually became more involved in the voluntary sector, working with the local branch of what was then the Marriage Guidance Council (now Relate), the PPA (Pre-school Playgroups Association) and helping to set up a drop-in centre for people with mental health problems. Ros had suffered sexual abuse as a child. At first she did not reveal her experiences; 'It wasn't something you could talk about in those days. I was concerned that people would not want their children to come to tea with my daughter.' She did eventually become involved in a group for survivors and started to address her own problem. She established herself as a positive voice for victims and aimed to raise awareness of the problem of child abuse. She was so successful in fundraising and promotion that she was soon much sought after by organisations in the field.

While facilitating one such group, she met two women who were on an Access Course. She herself had always wanted to study history but had never quite got round to it. When she heard about the Access Course, she thought, 'If they can do it so can I.' This was her inspiration. Another motivation was her desire to be 'on a level playing field' with the professionals she met in the course of her work. 'I felt my voice wasn't considered valid because I couldn't prove what I was saying academically.' At first she felt intimidated by formal education and tempted to drop out. As a mature student, it wasn't always possible for her to accept what was being taught; as she had developed her own ideas. However she persevered: 'I knew I was capable.' She was also motivated by the fact that others stuck it out.

Following completion of the Access Course, she decided to apply for a degree course and was accepted for Women's Studies and Social Administration at Roehampton Institute. When she first started studying, she tried to cram in everything: voluntary work, home life and study. Eventually the overload became so great that she fell victim to a viral heart infection and ended up in hospital. 'At this point I felt like giving up but, by then, I felt I had achieved too much to let it fall to waste.' She was able to return to college after a short rest. She felt restored but was determined not to get so overwhelmed in future. She managed to negotiate extensions on her work deadlines and, after a year of following the course part time (she didn't want full-time commitment because she had a ten-year-old daughter), she decided to go full time to qualify for fees and a grant. After this degree she wants to do an MSc, though money might prove a barrier. Her main ambition is to work in a Women's Centre where she would be able to support and encourage other women to organise and live their lives in the way they would like. For her own part, she feels she has achieved what she set out to do. 'I am equal to the professionals who used to "look down" on my opinions. Now I am able to argue back rather than to sit and accept. People know I have an equal argument. It's all about pursuing your own solutions and finding out what works for you.'

- 'Getting slim led to a new career.'
Linda Huett, vice president of Weight Watchers, UK.

After the birth of her three children, Linda ballooned by 5½ stone. She had always had a weight problem but now it was harder to diet because she was at home with the children and had developed a tendency to nibble. She decided she wanted to lose 3 stone and gave herself the target of losing it by the time her twins were a year old. Her motivation was that she did not feel like herself, carrying so much extra weight.

At first she tried to go it alone. However, by the twins' first birthday she had only succeeded in losing 1 stone, so she decided to join Weight Watchers. She liked the diet they proposed because it allowed her to eat well and yet still lose weight. She found the discipline of going to the weekly meetings helped to keep up her motivation. Between joining in September and the following January, she lost the extra 2 stone. She took it a week at a time, rewarding herself with a bowl of cornflakes with a sprinkle of sugar on a Sunday evening, if she had done well. To tone her body she exercised with a friend at each other's houses while their children were sleeping. She found this also helped her to keep on track: if one did not feel like exercising, the other talked her into it.

When she discovered that Weight Watchers were recruiting leaders she joined them on a part-time basis. As she had always been organised, she managed to work around her husband's hours and her children. Friends helped too. It took determination but she had missed having a job and adult contact. She gained a lot of satisfaction from working which kept her going when she felt like giving up. Although ideally she would have liked to wait until her twins had started school, when a full-time opportunity came up, she decided to go for it. 'Such opportunities don't always come along when you want them.' She was confident that she could do the job and believed that, 'Although you don't always get what you want, you must try.' The extra income allowed her to employ a Nanny, and, despite having to turn down a couple of promotions, her career snowballed. Three and a half years ago she become general manager for the UK and two years later vice president. She says, 'I love my work and find the company stimulating.' She believes that to succeed you need a realistic idea of your stamina and of what you can achieve, together with the support and understanding of those at home.

SOME BOOKS YOU MAY FIND ENCOURAGING:

- **Work and life management**

What Color is Your Parachute. Richard Nelson Bolles, Ten Speed Press.
Build Your Own Rainbow. Barry Hopson and Mike Scally, Management Books 2000 Ltd.
The Personal Managment Handbook. How to Make the Most of Your Potential. John Mulligan, Marshall Editions.

- **Relationships**

Love Strategies. Ian Grove-Stephensen and Susan Quilliam, Thorsons.
The Good Relationship Guide. Dr Maryon Tysoe, Piatkus.

- **Appearance**

The Y Plan Physical. Jill Gaskell and Dr Craig Sharp, Hamlyn.
Beautiful Body. Beautiful Skin. Norma Knox, Piatkus.
Vogue More Dash Than Cash. Linda Watson and Rosie Martin. Conde Nast Books.

- **Health and Longevity**

The Ace Plan. The Secrets of Living Younger Longer. Liz Earle, Boxtree.
Look Younger. Feel Better. Dr James Scala and Barbara Jacques, Piatkus.

- **Personal growth and self esteem**

Your Perfect Right. Robert Alberti and Michael Emmons, Impact.
A Picture of Health. How to Use Guided Imagery for Self-Healing and Personal Growth. Helen Graham, Piatkus.
The Positive Woman. Gael Lindenfield, Thorsons.
The Road Less Travelled. M. Scott Peck, Arrow.

USEFUL ADDRESSES

How to get what you want out of life

There are numerous organisations and individuals offering lifeskills and personal development training. Your local education authority (LEA) will be able to give details of ones in your area. You can also pick up a prospectus at your local library, or you could try the Workers' Educational Association in your area. Other useful addresses include:

Human Potential Resource Group
Department of Education Studies
University of Surrey
Guildford
GU2 5XH
Tel: (01483) 300800

John Seymour Associates Ltd INLP
17 Boyce Drive
Bristol
BS2 9XQ
Tel: (0117) 955 7827

The Isis Centre
262 High Road
Tottenham
London N17
Tel: (0181) 808 6401

The Open University
Walton Hall
Milton Keynes
MK7 6AA

How to get what you want out of work

Ask your local library or CAB to provide you with details of careers counsellors in your area. Specific job vacancies in the UK and abroad can be found in:

Jobs in Europe
52 Queens Garden
London
W2 3AA

Overseas Jobs Express
Island Publishing
PO Box 22
Brighton
BN1 6HX
Tel: (01273) 440220

New Ways to Work
Upper Street
London
N1 OPD
Tel: (0171) 226 4026
(Information about job-sharing)

Part-time Careers Ltd
10 Golden Square
London
W1R 2AF
(0171) 437 3103/734 0559

Industrial Common Ownership Movement
Vassalli House
20 Central Road
Leeds
LS1 6DE
Tel: (01132) 461737
(How to set up a worker-run cooperative)

Business in the Community
8 Statham Street
London
W1X 6AH
Tel: (0171) 629 1600
(Information about self-employment and enterprise agencies in your area)

National Council for Voluntary Organisations
Regent's Wharf
8 All Saints Street
London
N1 9RL
Tel: (0171) 713 6161

How to get what you want out of your relationship

Relate (formerly Marriage Guidance Council)
11 Church Street
Rugby
CV21 3AW
Tel: (01788) 565 675

British Association of Counselling
Reagent's Place
Rugby
CV21 2PJ
Tel: (01788) 578 328

How to look the way you want

Weight Watchers UK
Kidwells Park House
Kidwells Park Drive
Maidenhead
SL6 8YT
Tel: (01628) 777 077

Cosmetic Surgery Network
Cindy Jackson
PO Box 3410
London
N6 4EE
Tel: (0181) 983 3567

INDEX

abdomen 160
action plan, developing 33–7, 104, 165
  financial 64, 65–6
  proceeding with 37–40, 118–19
action, positive 35
agendas, hidden 80
AHAs (alphahydroxy acids) 158
alcohol 162
Alberti, Robert E. 182
appearance, personal 24, 37, 149–60 see also clothes
Argyle, Michael 24
assets, personal 36, 66
attention, gaining 77–8
attitudes 46

barriers 88–98
  overcoming 138–44
beliefs 13, 23, 26, 46
  dangerous 139
blood pressure test 171
blueprint, genetic 9
BMI (body mass index) 153
body clock 45
body language 37, 39, 70, 73, 75, 85, 143
BPH (benign prostatic hypertrophy) 176
brain, left side 4
  right side 4
brainstorming 14, 32, 65, 142, 150
breasts 157
  cancer see cancer, breast
  examination of 173–4
  implants, silicon 158
Burgess, Anthony 47
business, unfinished 10

calories 155
cancer, breast 173 see also mammography
  cervical 177 see also smear, cervical
  ovarian 178
  skin 172, 178
  testicular 176
capital 58
career 23
  developing 120–1
  guidance 119–20
Carlisle, Thomas 155
change 33, 42–55, 135, 139
  fear of 89–90
check-up, dental 172
childhood 59
children 60
choice 35, 44
cholesterol 171
clothes 75, 155–6
communication 70–87
confidence 30, 148
Conran, Shirley 67
control 25
cost-benefit analysis 20, 150
courage 201
creativity 26, 112

Daly, Barbara 152
debt 64, 67–8
decision-making 144
dermabrasion 159
desire, negative 4
  positive 4
development, personal 26, 180–5
dieting 148, 154–5
disappointment, dealing with 186–7
dreams 16–17, 18, 19, 30–41, 181, 186, 192
  and reality 110
dress, style of see clothes

ectomorph 152
Eliot, T.S. 197
emotions 12, 104, 190
  dealing with 186–8
endomorph 152
energy 30, 46
excuses 90–1
exercise 148, 155, 157, 158, 162, 195

face 158–60
  lift 159
fantasies 15
feelings see emotions
fitness 155, 164
flexibility 98
focusing 30, 31, 139

gains 20
genes 163–4
genetic blueprint see blueprint, genetic
goals 20, 33, 42, 49, 186
  setting 30, 34–6, 46–7, 133, 151
  short-term 35
  structuring 36–7
gratification, deferred 2
growth, personal see development, personal

happiness 24, 195
health 25–6, 37, 161–79
  checks 171 see also well-person check; well-woman check
heart 175
  disease 175, 178
history, personal 8

identity, sense of 27
imagination 4, 15, 30, 167–8, 181
  guided 15
impotence 176

income 58, 63–4
infertility 176
information 62
  gathering 31, 32
inspiration 30
  people 27–8
intuition 4

Jackson, Michael 150

knowledge 31

language, 'I' 144
laughter 104, 195
lid lift 159
life, attitudes towards 37
  personal meaning in 26
  plan 53
lifeline 12
lifestyle 58
liposuction 156, 160
listening, good 82–5
logic 4
longevity 25–6, 162 see also health
losers 94 see also thinking, negative
losses 20
love, romantic 127

mammography 174
marriage 24
massage 158
meditation 195
mesomorph 152
messages, *should* and *ought* 20, 52
money 27, 40, 56–9 see also capital; income
motivation 6, 19, 30, 35, 49, 114, 139, 155, 167
motivators 23, 27

National Fitness Survey 166
needs, basic survival 21
  emotional 21
  physical 21
  spiritual 21, 181

nerve growth factors 171
networking 120
non-verbal
  communication *see* body language
'non-verbal leakage' 76

optimism 96
osteoporosis 168, 174
outgoings 63

past, breaking from 93
Peale, Norman Vincent 98
penis 176
personality,
  'administrator' 113
  'doer' 111
  'entrepreneur' 114
  creative 112
  states 10
  'thinker' 112
  traits 10
pessimism 96
  defensive 100
'possible self' 15
prioritising 47–9, 52
problem-solving
  technique 141
progress 30, 33
  monitoring 47, 123, 169

reality 19, 30–41
relationships 24, 62, 126–47, 180
  happy 138
  unhappy 138
resources 36, 44
retirement 60–1
rhinoplasty 159–60

Satir, Virginia 93
self-actualisation 26
self-confidence 56, 196
self-disclosure 86
self-employment 121–2
  see also work

self-esteem 23, 24, 25, 27, 42, 52, 142, 150, 194
self-image 75
self-knowledge 6, 35
self-respect 23
sex 24
shyness 10
skills, transferable 116
smear, cervical 173
smoking 162, 177
sociability 10
sperm count 176
stomach 175
strategies, coping 99
  winning 99
strength 37
subtasks 36
success 27, 35
support 190
surgery, cosmetic 148, 156–7, 158

thighs 160
thinking, lateral 32
  negative 13, 95, 100, 191
  positive 98, 139, 195
thought 12
  losing *see* thinking, negative
time 37, 40, 90
  management of 42–55
  wasters 51

values 23, 26
visualisation 15–8, 145, 167

weight 163
  losing 152, 155 see also dieting
well-person check 171
well-woman check 172–3
willpower 19
winners 94 see also thinking, positive
work 23, 61 see also self-employment
  getting 110–25